Transforming Lives
Through Personal Storytelling

Hippie Boy Teaching Guide

By Marjie Bowker

With Assistance from Ingrid Ricks

Transforming Lives Through Personal Storytelling
Hippie Boy Teaching Guide

Book layout by Hydra House
www.hydrahousebooks.com

By Marjie Bowker
With Assistance from Ingrid Ricks

For more information, visit: www.WriteToRight.org

Table of Contents

FOREWORD

Using the power of students' stories, Marjie Bowker and Ingrid Ricks have created a rigorous and engaging curriculum that increases self-efficacy and resiliency, teaches higher order thinking skills, touches students' hearts and souls, and transforms as it informs, all with an eye on the Common Core State Standards.

If you are looking for a curriculum designed to give students voice, this is it. After seeing the transformations in their students at Scriber Lake High School in Edmonds, Washington, they created this wonderful gift so others could have the same life-changing experiences.

Use it to teach, to inspire and most of all, to enjoy!

Cal Crow, Ph. D.
Center for Learning Connections
Center for Efficacy and Resiliency
Edmonds Community College

This writing project has transformed the lives of Scriber Lake students. It has freed the writers from burdens of the past and has enabled them to move on with their lives. It has also changed the lives of the students who have witnessed the courage of their peers and who desired the end result of freedom for themselves.

Even though I interact with these students on a daily basis, reading their stories has given me a depth of understanding for who they are—what they've been through and their resiliency. It makes me want to do everything I can to help them realize their dreams and goals so that they can have the futures they deserve.

The curriculum developed by Marjie Bowker and Ingrid Ricks has captured even the most reluctant writers, inspiring them to revise draft after draft of their stories. The skills they have learned has also enabled them to gain confidence in writing overall and, as a result, many of them achieved success on the writing standards required by Washington State.

I highly recommend this study guide as a tool for educators who want to make a difference in their students' lives.

Kathy Clift
Principal, Scriber Lake High School
Edmonds, Washington

WHY WE STARTED THIS PROGRAM

A Note From Ingrid Ricks

It was my own struggle with the pain I'd carried inside of me for years—followed by my ultimate decision to write and publish my memoir—that made me understand the life-changing power of personal storytelling.

I'd tried to write my memoir, *Hippie Boy: A Girl's Story*—about my childhood struggles to escape an abusive stepfather and the extreme religion and poverty at home—for more than a decade. But the emotions bottled inside me were so painful that I cried every time I opened my computer to write. I decided it was easier just to keep the hurt safely tucked away.

Then, in late January 2004, I was diagnosed with Retinitis Pigmentosa, an incurable degenerative eye disease that is slowly stealing my eyesight. In my quest to save my vision, I sought treatment from a doctor who focuses on whole body health. He kicked off my appointment by asking me to tell him about my childhood. Within minutes, I was sobbing.

The doctor told me it was clear I was carrying around a huge negative energy charge over something that happened so many years ago. Then he added, "If you don't think that carrying this inside of you is impacting your physical health, you're crazy."

The idea that holding onto the anguish from all those years ago could actually be causing me to go blind was a huge wake up call for me. I finally decided to confront my emotions and write my book, and discovered the immense healing power and validation that comes from getting the words out on paper. I also started openly sharing my story through essays and podcasts and discovered something else: that I wasn't alone in my experiences and that by sharing my story with the world, I was making connections and giving others a voice.

Even before publishing *Hippie Boy*, I knew I wanted to use my story to help teenagers who were struggling with similar issues to reclaim their power and move on with their lives. So when Marjie Bowker contacted me about using my book, I felt like I was being handed a huge gift.

What started as a month-long unit that used *Hippie Boy* as a guide to help Marjie's students find their voice and power by writing their personal stories has since turned into a comprehensive writing program. Our collaboration has so far led to three published student story collections and a life-changing experience for the student authors involved. It has also led to the launch of our youth storytelling organization, WriteToRight.org, and a joint commitment to share this program with educators and mentors so more youth can experience the transformational power of personal storytelling.

A Note from Marjie Bowker

Making my students into published authors was not on my mind in the fall of 2011 when I first read Ingrid Ricks' memoir; I was just happy to find a book that I knew they would love. But when I learned the story behind Ingrid's story—that it wasn't until she gave herself permission to write her story and share it with others that she was able to let go of the pain from her childhood– I knew my students deserved that same opportunity.

Ingrid started coming into my English classes to discuss *Hippie Boy* and to ask one question of my students: "What is your story?" And despite the issues that were constantly interfering with their education—homelessness, poverty, abuse and drug and alcohol issues—they became fully engaged in answering that question.

Today, as a result of our partnership, we have published three story collections: *We Are Absolutely Not Okay, You've Got it All Wrong*, and *Behind Closed Doors: Stories from the Inside Out*. We have seen individual lives, our school and our connection to the community transform. And we have watched our students become writers—many of whom had no previous confidence, or interest, in writing. These students, and their books, are proof that most students absolutely want to write.

Relevance used to be my biggest concern as a teacher; now, however, my students read their stories publicly every chance they get: in front of their peers, at other schools, at local Rotary and Kiwanis Club meetings, at local bookstores and conferences. Last fall we adapted three stories for the stage in a partnership with Seattle Public Theater, and Edmonds Community College chose *You've Got it All Wrong* as their "Community Read" for the 2014-15 school year. My students now view themselves as participants in a universal dialogue—participants who are making a difference in other people's lives.

This curriculum, which adheres to the Common Core State Standards for Narrative Writing, is the product of Ingrid's and my journey together, helping students to identify their stories and guiding them through multiple drafts to make every detail count. What I have learned through this process is that all students have stories to tell, and that struggling writers need a different, personal and engaging approach to inspire them.

Now, at Scriber Lake High School, we write our own stories. We hope that this guide will help you and your students enter into that dialogue along with us.

What Students Are Saying

Aydan Dennis, 14

Hippie Boy helped me to find out that it's okay to share your thoughts and feelings of intense personal moments and abusive life stories to others, and that sharing such can teach others. Writing my story helped me because it allowed me to release pent-up frustration without hurting others, and lifted a weight off my shoulders. It helped me to reveal other feelings I had about what I wrote, and helped me to realize that it's okay to share this story with others.

Tattiyana Fernandez, 17

When I read the first chapter of *Hippie Boy*, it got me so hyped up! I could relate to Ingrid and how she felt. It brought back so many emotions and feelings from my experience with my step dad. Because of the way Ingrid wrote her story, I felt like I was there. It really pushed me to write my deepest secret and get my story out there. Writing my story has been a huge achievement for me! It honestly is the best thing I could have done. It has helped me overcome so many of my problems, because until then I thought I was the only one who struggled with abandonment. Knowing that my deepest story can help someone is the best feeling in the world to me.

Emmasariah Jensen, 14

Reading *Hippie Boy* helped me write my story because I read about how Ingrid went through things that I went through, too. I grew up in a Mormon family with an irresponsible father and felt trapped in a world I wanted to escape from so badly. Ingrid found her voice and her freedom. She proved that it wasn't easy, that sometimes everything just goes to hell. Knowing this, I was able to get my feelings out after holding them in my whole life. Writing my story helped me get all of my feelings out because I've never told anybody any of my feelings about how and who I was raised by. I feel so relieved and I feel as if it's okay to feel the emotions I've held in so long.

Kai Lee, 14

Reading *Hippie Boy* helped me because when we were writing our stories and needed to show emotion, we could refer back to see how *Hippie Boy* was written. I don't know why but it made school feel more relaxing.

Vasilly Karpinskiy, 14

After finishing the book I wondered, "What is the point of hiding something that makes you feel bad for years?" The way writing my story helped me: well, I definitely did lose a lot of stress and now that a few people know, they are helping me get over it.

Michael Coffman, 14

Hippie Boy inspired me to write my story because it's a true story written by someone who went through difficult situations. It was powerful to read through these events from Ingrid's point of view. Writing my story helped me let go of what happened and took away a lot of anger and resentment.

Shelby Asbury, 15

Reading *Hippie Boy* helped me write my story because Ingrid puts so much heart into her story that it makes me know that it's okay to write about my life. Ingrid writes with so much emotion and explains everything that happened to her. Her story made me think, if she can do it, why can't I? Writing my own story had its pros and cons. Although writing it helped me sort through emotions that I needed to deal with, it brought up memories I didn't want to face. In the long run it helped me because getting my story out helped me get over my fear of my abuser. Writing my story helped me heal a little faster. I cried a couple of times while writing it, and sometimes writing ruined my whole entire day. But to this day it's helping me because I got everything I've been holding in out.

Destiny Allison, 17

Reading *Hippie Boy* helped me understand that nobody has a perfect life and everybody has a story - it's just a matter of getting that story out. The *Hippie Boy* Study Guide gave me the chance to pull apart pieces of the story and analyze them so that I could add effective details to my own story.

SUGGESTIONS FOR TEACHING HIPPIE BOY

The overall goal of this curriculum is for students to identify the narrative writing techniques used in *Hippie Boy* and then to apply them when they write their own narrative scenes. Students will easily engage with the story, which makes breaking down the narrative techniques fun.

Students of all ages will connect with *Hippie Boy*, but Ingrid and I have discovered that the "sweet spot" is for 9th and 10th graders; developmentally, they are at the same stage that Ingrid was when she experienced her most extreme hardships. To journey with her through them to a place where she finds her own strength and freedom is especially good for the soul of a fourteen or fifteen year-old.

Below are some suggestions based on how I have taught this unit, which lasts between four and five weeks for my classes:

Reading *Hippie Boy* out loud:

Because *Hippie Boy* contains such vivid characters and is mainly a scene-based memoir, students enjoy reading it out loud, almost like a play (Reader's Theater style). I read as "narrator"—everything that isn't in quotes—and then assign reading parts. My students usually compete to read the part of "Earl" or "Dad," and one male student nailed the voice of Ingrid's mother, using the "t" sound for all "d's" to create an Austrian accent. It won't take long for students to get the flow of this type of reading literature. Reading out loud enables all students to engage in the reading and perform at differing levels of comfort while increasing comprehension and reading motivation.

Be sure to read the first chapter out loud because this allows students—as a group—to experience Ingrid's feelings of powerlessness, sets the tone for her struggles to come and energizes the class. Because I teach generally low readers, we read (at least) the first five chapters out loud to ensure comprehension.

Other scenes that work especially well read out loud:

- The cake scene in chapter 3
- The meeting with Bishop Jones in chapter 10
- The father-daughter meeting scene in chapter 12
- The climax where Ingrid saves her dad in the courtroom in chapter 15

I write the parts on the board and choose volunteers, like this:

- Earl- Aydan
- Ingrid—Shelby
- Dad—Dylan
- Ingrid's Mom—Zack

Small Dramatic Sketches

Many of the chapter sections include dramatic scenes written in play format with dialogue taken directly from the book. My students really enjoy acting out the scenes—especially any scenes that involve Earl. If you have active kids in your classes, these small sketches are a great tool to get them up and moving around while connecting with the emotions in the story.

The "Fictional Stories" in chapter 2 (for Ingrid's mother's backstory) and in chapter 14 (when Ingrid's dad is held hostage):

I find that giving students words to make up their own story about a character creates interest in the true story. After they write and read their own stories out loud (which are often very funny), their interest is heightened and they retain much more information from the chapter. This writing activity never fails to draw my students in—they love to make outlandish tales out of the words provided to them.

HELPING STUDENTS TO IDENTIFY AND WRITE THEIR STORIES

Our opening question is always "What is your story?" Many can answer this immediately, while some begin by saying that they don't have a story. However, as soon as they read a few chapters from *Hippie Boy* or excerpts from our student stories (included in this guide) from *We Are Absolutely Not Okay, You've Got it All Wrong*, and *Behind Closed Doors: Stories from the Inside Out*, a light switches on inside of them.

These scenes and stories cover issues that are common in many students' lives: abandonment, divorce, poverty, power struggles, abuse and feelings of helplessness. By using these and then incorporating related questions as writing prompts, students quickly begin to identify their own personal experiences. Overall, students appreciate the "no specific prompt" approach. "It's up to you what story you are going to tell" works a lot better than "Write about a life-changing experience" because of the freedom it allows.

What we've discovered is that when given a guide to follow and an opportunity to share, students become engaged with their hearts and souls, and narrative writing no longer feels like work to them.

Writing "In Scene":

It's a big challenge to get students to narrow their stories into just one scene and to write it in the moment—to "show" instead of "tell" the story. Many tend to want to write about a string of events that happened over a long period of time.

To help students understand the concept of a scene, the "Scene Construction" charts included for chapters 1, 10, 15 and 16 are extremely helpful. We also read stories from our student books and then discuss how much real time was involved in each one (in addition to all of the other topics that spring from them). All of our published writers worked hard to narrow their stories down to be told in-the-moment, so most of them take place in under a half an hour – some within just minutes. Most scenes include flashbacks or background information to provide context and to help deepen the story arc, but they are placed within the real time of the event that is happening.

We also place a high importance on individual student/teacher conferences (about ten-minutes in length) to help students visualize the scene before they begin to write. Soon we hear students asking each other, "Does this take place in under a half an hour?" If the answer is "no," then they might brainstorm how the insertion of a flashback would help focus the story.

Another constant discussion involves how "painting" the setting, characters, dialogue, emotions and sensory details (SCEDS) into the story will slow it down in order to invite readers into the experience. I repeatedly remind my students of the "Broken Necks, Blank Minds" activity because it helps them to remember that they are transferring a unique experience into the mind of a person who has no concept of what actually happened. Sometimes they ask to do this activity again for an active break from writing because they enjoy it so much.

SCEDS (Setting, Character, Emotion, Dialogue, Sensory Detail) Lesson Plans:

Before any formal scene-writing takes place, I make sure my students have been given many opportunities to practice writing "in scene."

The SCEDS lessons are designed to remove obstacles for reluctant writers by providing them with the building blocks necessary to construct descriptions of characters, settings, emotions and dialogue through the use of sensory details. Once they have the words, their ideas will flow freely. Students respond well to visual cues and quickly engage with their emotions—and these lessons invite them to do so. I have been using these techniques in my classroom for the past four years and cannot recall many refusals to participate; usually, even my least confident writers will become engaged and share their writing with the class. Most of the examples included in the SCEDS lessons are written by ninth graders – most of whom have had little success within the school system.

When students are ready to begin writing their scenes (after practicing with the basic SCEDS lessons), I usually start the process by having them use the "Your Narrative Scene – SETTING" chart to help them to write themselves into the real-time setting of their story. Once they are in-the-moment, they will usually stay there.

Although the focus is on the use of visuals, adding other sensory experiences will enhance them even further; when you can, add sounds, tastes, textures and scents. The more students engage with their senses, the more engaged they will be with writing.

Free-Writing in Response to Stories and Prompts:

Throughout this process, allow time for students to free-write their responses to stories and/or prompts; after completing the readings they are usually full of connections, so try to utilize that energy while it's at a high level.

I require between a half and a whole page of writing for each free-writing session (usually around 10-15 minutes). I have no rules for this, other than "write." I don't grade them, except for quantity, and I usually comment on them and suggest stories that spring from a portion of what they've written—often the real stories are hidden somewhere in the rambling. The most honest writing usually comes from the time that I allow them to "free write" in class.

The Formal Narrative Scene Assignment:

After reading the first few chapters of *Hippie Boy*, reading scenes out loud from our student books and discussing them ("What did this writer do well? How did he or she "paint" this scene to make it come alive? How did the structure work in real time?"), practicing writing techniques through use of the SCEDS, many free-writes, and our ten-minute student/teacher conferences, students are practically begging to begin writing their scenes. As mentioned above, beginning with the "Your Narrative Scene – SETTING" chart will set them on the right path.

After the "first final draft" (what I call it), we work on the blending techniques and structural elements so they can be applied to their second and third drafts. (Suggested schedule included later.)

Assessment:

I use the Common Core State Standards Narrative Writing Rubric to assess the formal narrative scene assignment:

http://www.schoolimprovement.com/docs/Common%20Core%20Rubrics_Gr9-10.pdf

Considerations Regarding Students' Stories

I am very fortunate to have a competent counseling staff at my disposal; students know that if they write about a traumatic event in my class, they will be connected with an appropriate professional. If I could not depend on this support, I would hesitate to invite this type of honesty—it's a lot of responsibility, and I am not a counselor. However, over and over again, the act of objectifying these experiences through writing creates a community of understanding made up of strong individual voices. Many students express that this is the most surprisingly effective "therapy" they have ever experienced.

Some begin the writing process saying, "I'm just going to write this for myself." Some of these students change their minds and proceed to the publishing phase, while some who intend to publish decide against that step in the end. We let them set their own rules and view ourselves as guides for the process.

We also offer the choice of using a pen name. One student was afraid of gang retaliation the first year, but the second year he was ready to use his real name. Another was still in the home where her abuse scene occurred and waivered over this decision. In the end she decided to use it so that the truth of what happened was really told. Each student must consider the consequences of making a story public, and must be guided well in making that decision.

We encourage students to communicate honestly with their parents about the content of their stories (and, of course, we have students and parents sign waiver forms); however, often that is the most difficult conversation to have and it doesn't always happen.

At our first book release party, a parent approached me and said, "You know more about my daughter than I do. I hope you are prepared to provide the counseling we need over this." Her comment shook me, and I told her that our counseling staff would be happy to set an appointment with the two of them. A few days later, she told me that she and her daughter had been able to discuss her story in the past week and that they had never before shared such open communication. She admitted to feeling exposed by the story, but in the end, she expressed gratitude for the exposure because of the good it did their relationship.

When I first started this endeavor, I was uneasy about the responsibilities involved. But now I know that the benefits far outweigh the trouble. Students who desire the freedom that comes from getting their stories out and who are courageous enough to initiate that process are the reward for all the work it requires to facilitate the process.

Students as Teachers

The most rewarding part of this process is when students begin conferencing with each other on their own time, asking for and offering advice regarding how to clarify each other's stories. My students are now helping to teach these concepts in the classrooms and seminars where they present their stories; they have come full circle and are now teaching others as they continue to strengthen their own writing skills.

Suggested Schedule for Teaching Hippie Boy

My classes meet for an 85-minute period every day and this unit lasts between four and five weeks for my students (including at least three revisions of their narrative scenes—at their request). Below is my suggestion for the order of when to use each part of this curriculum. One schedule is for teaching *Hippie Boy* and the other is for teaching narrative writing; I mix the two together, but have separated them here so that teachers can mix and match according to their classroom schedules and chemistries.

Week One:

1. Read chapter 1 out loud—Reader's Theater Style

2. Chapter 1, questions for discussion/free writing response

3. Study guide, chapter 1, questions 1-4

4. Artistic response to chapter one

5. Small Sketch, "Earl Says No"—(to review chapter 1 before moving on to chapter 2)

6. Chapter 2—students write character backstory for Ingrid's mother

7. Read chapter 2 out loud – Reader's Theater Style

8. Chapter 2, questions for discussion/free writing response

9. Study guide, chapter 2

10. Read chapters 3 & 4 (read cake scene out loud)

11. Chapters 3 & 4, questions for discussion/free writing response

12. Study guide, chapters 3 & 4

Week Two:

13. Small Sketch, "Ingrid and the Cake" (to review chapters 3 & 4 before moving on)

14. Read chapters 5 & 6

15. Chapters 5 & 6, questions for discussion/free writing response

16. Study guide, chapters 5 & 6

17. Chapters 7, 8 & 9 vocabulary

18. Read chapters 7, 8 & 9

19. Chapters 7, 8 & 9, questions for discussion/free writing response

20. Study guide, chapters 7, 8 & 9

Week Three

21. Read chapters 10 & 11

22. Chapters 10 & 11 questions for discussion/free writing response

23. Study guide, chapters 10 & 11

24. Small sketch: "Father/Daughter Meeting" (to review chapters 10 & 11 before moving on)

25. Chapters 12 & 13 vocabulary

26. Read chapters 12 & 13

27. Chapters 12 & 13 questions for discussion/free writing response

28. Study guide, chapters 12 & 13

29. Chapters 14 & 15 vocabulary

30. Read chapters 14 & 15

31. Chapters 14 & 15 questions for discussion/free writing response

32. Study guide, chapters 14 & 15

Week Four

33. Small sketches: "Dad's Kidnapping" and "Ingrid Finds Her Voice" (to review chapters 14 & 15 before moving on)

34. Chapters 16, 17 & 18 vocabulary

35. Read chapters 16, 17 & 18

36. Chapters 16, 17 & 18 questions for discussion/free writing response

37. Study guide, chapters 14 & 15

Week Five

38. Draft, peer edit, final edits of narrative scene

SUGGESTED SCHEDULE FOR TEACHING NARRATIVE WRITING

Part One: Identify Stories

Read scenes written by other student writers, free-write responses, hold ten-minute conferences.

Ask students: "What is your story?" or "What are your stories?" "Which one do you want to tell and how do you want to tell it?"

When your students have identified their stories, move on to Part Two:

Part Two: Practice Writing and Transfer Skills to Actual Scenes for Pre-Writing

Suggested Order of Lesson Plans:

1. **Pre-writing Lesson: Broken Necks/Blank Minds.**

   Establishes a general mindset regarding the transference of a unique story from one person to another and the necessity to "paint" it well into the other person's mind.

2. **SCEDS Lesson One – Writing with Sensory Detail.**

   Establishes the use of sensory detail writing in-the-moment (for all of the writing to come).

3. **SCEDS Lesson Two: Setting – Painting a Place with Words.**

   This lesson presents writers with compelling settings that are fun to imagine and write about.

4. **SCEDS Lesson Three: Character – Painting a Portrait with Words.**

   This lesson Invites writers to recognize many facets of character description.

5. **SCEDS Lesson Four, Emotional/Physical Response.**

   This lesson elicits the most heart-and-soul writing because it is emotion–based. It's interesting to see what stories come out of the brainstorming activity because students quickly identify their most intense emotional experiences.

6. **SCEDS Lesson Five: Dialogue–Bringing Scenes to Life with Dialogue, Blocking and Emotion.**

   This lesson is fun for students because by this time they will have the confidence to use all of the SCEDS elements to paint an entire short scene.

7. **Your Narrative Scene, SETTING (Brainstorming Chart).**

   Using the skills they have just practiced, writers will place themselves in-the-moment of the scene they are writing. If writers begin here, it's easier to stay in-scene as they continue. Some writers will have only one setting, but many will have more than one. Help them brainstorm the primary location from which the rest of the story unfolds and work with that until it is established. When it is time to go to the flashback or the next setting, your writers will transition with more ease. (With some groups, this is the only chart I use from the "Your Narrative Scene" section; others need the additional help to transition from the practice concepts to the actual scene-writing.)

8. **Your Narrative Scene, CHARACTER (Brainstorming Chart).**

   Using the skills they have just practiced, writers will be able to paint their own characters into their stories with vivid detail.

9. **Your Narrative Scene, EMOTIONS (Brainstorming Chart).**

   Using the skills they have just practiced, writers will be able to identify and write about strong emotional responses within their scenes.

10. **Your Narrative Scene, DIALOGUE & EMOTIONAL RESPONSE (Brainstorming Chart).**

    Writing one small scene successfully will spark students' ideas about where to add dialogue in their own scenes.

Part Two (B): Polishing the SCEDS

For extended work on the SCEDS elements, the following lessons work really well to solidify what was learned in the basic lessons:

1. SCEDS Lesson Two (B): Blending Setting Descriptions into Narratives

2. SCEDS Lesson Three (B): Blending Character Descriptions into Narratives

3. SCEDS Lesson Four (B): Adding Emotional/Physical Response

4. SCEDS Lesson Five (B): Bringing Scenes to Life with Dialogue, Blocking and Emotion

Part Three: Write the First Final Draft

Using their "Your Narrative Scene" charts and written responses, students will be able to begin piecing together their scenes with confidence.

Part Four: Edit First Final Drafts

At times, I use the Part Two (B) SCEDS lessons at this editing stage if I didn't get the chance before. However, I always save the following lesson for the final edit:

1. SCENE CONSTRUCTION Lesson One: Using Flashbacks to Sequence Events in a Scene

2. SCENE CONSTRUCTION Lesson Two: Sequencing Events in a Scene

3. SCENE CONSTRUCTION Lesson Three: Engaging the Reader

   If I teach this lesson too early, students get confused and are hesitant to write. When I teach it after the first draft, lights go on quickly regarding how to make their leads more compelling.

Part Five: Final Drafts/Sharing

I usually hold class readings at the end of this unit, and am always surprised by how many decide to share their stories. I place a stool and a lamp in front of the class – and bring cookies –and invite them to come up to read when "the spirit moves" them. I never require this, but many decide to take that step when they witness the courage of their peers (sometimes a little extra credit is highly motivating, too). These readings have been the highlight for many of my classes. (If students are writing deep, painful stories of abuse, I am especially careful about inviting them to read. By the end of this process, our counselors are aware of the students who are writing about traumatic events and have spoken with them about this issue.)

CURRICULUM GUIDE TO COMMON CORE STATE STANDARDS: NARRATIVE WRITING

Standard:	Lessons in the *Hippie Boy Teaching Guide* tied to this standard:
CCSS.ELA-Literacy.W.9-10.3d Use precise words and phrases, telling details, and sensory language to convey a vivid picture of the experiences, events, setting, and/or characters.	SCEDS Lesson One: Identifying Sensory Details SCEDS Lesson Two: Painting a Portrait with Words SCEDS Lesson Three: Painting a Place with Words
CCSS.ELA-Literacy.W.9-10.3b Use narrative techniques, such as dialogue, pacing, description, reflection, and multiple plot lines, to develop experiences, events, and/or characters.	SCEDS Lesson Four: Adding Dialogue and Blocking to a Scene SCEDS Lesson Five: Writing to Convey the Physical Impact of Emotions
CCSS.ELA-Literacy.W.9-10.3c Use a variety of techniques to sequence events so that they build on one another to create a coherent whole.	SCENE CONSTRUCTION Lesson One: Using Flashbacks to Sequence Events in a Scene SCENE CONSTRUCTION Lesson Two: Sequencing Events in a Scene
CCSS.ELA-Literacy.W.9-10.3a Engage and orient the reader by setting out a problem, situation, or observation, establishing one or multiple point(s) of view, and introducing a narrator and/or characters; create a smooth progression of experiences or events.	SCENE CONSTRUCTION Lesson Three: Engaging the Reader

Common Core State Standards for Reading Literature that are targeted throughout this guide:

CCSS.ELA-LITERACY.RL.9-10.1

Cite strong and thorough textual evidence to support analysis of what the text says explicitly as well as inferences drawn from the text.

CCSS.ELA-LITERACY.RL.9-10.2

Determine a theme or central idea of a text and analyze in detail its development over the course of the text, including how it emerges and is shaped and refined by specific details; provide an objective summary of the text.

CCSS.ELA-LITERACY.RL.9-10.3

Analyze how complex characters (e.g., those with multiple or conflicting motivations) develop over the course of a text, interact with other characters, and advance the plot or develop the theme.

CCSS.ELA-LITERACY.RL.9-10.5

Analyze how an author's choices concerning how to structure a text, order events within it (e.g., parallel plots), and manipulate time (e.g., pacing, flashbacks) create such effects as mystery, tension, or surprise.

DEFINITIONS

Narrative Writing

Narrative writing tells others the stories of our personal experiences and places them within the context of a larger theme, such as a lesson learned.

SCEDS

SCEDS are the building blocks used to create vivid narrative stories. Good narrative writing techniques invite readers to enter into our experience with us and can be broken down into the following five elements:

S—SETTING

C—CHARACTER

E—EMOTIONS

D—DIALOGUE

S—SENSORY DETAILS (sprinkled into all of the above elements)

NARRATIVE SCENES USING SCEDS

Assignment: Write a three-to-five page scene from your life—a piece that begins to reveal the story within your life story. Use the following SCEDS and Structural Elements to make your scene come to life:

_____**1. Setting**

- When and where does the scene take place?

- What is the environment like?

- What sensory details can you use to describe it?

_____**2. Character**

- What do your characters look, smell and sound like?

- What are your characters wearing?

- What are the ages of your characters?

- What are your characters' personality characteristics (loud, quiet, assertive)?

- What are your characters' backgrounds?

_____**3. Emotional/physical response**

- How do you feel during this scene?

- What happens to you physically when you experience these feelings?

- What is going on inside your head during this scene (your thoughts or inner dialogue)?

_____**4. Dialogue**

- What are you and your characters saying in your scene?

- What are you and your characters doing while you are talking? (blocking)

- What kind of body language is being used?

_____**5. Sensory Details (sprinkled into all of the above)**

- Visual (what you see)

- Auditory (what you hear)

- Kinesthetic (body language)

- Smell/Taste

SCENE CONSTRUCTION ELEMENTS

When writing your scene, also remember to keep these structural elements in mind:

_____**1. Story Arc**

- What happens in your story that takes a reader from point "a" to point "b"?

- What message do you want the reader to take away?

_____**2. Compelling Opening Sentence**

- What sentence will immediately grab readers and pull them into your story?

- Does your opening sentence have action?

  Passive opening sentence: I opened the door and saw Earl standing on the porch

  Active opening sentence: I should have slammed the door in Earl's face.

_____**3. Conflict/Action**

- What is the conflict/action in your scene?

- What happens that sets your scene in motion? Does someone get into a fight? Do you get in trouble with an adult?

_____**4. Context/backstory/flashback**

- What is the context of this scene?

- What paragraphs add necessary background information for the present action to make sense?

- Are there any flashbacks?

_____**5. Ending**

- What is the conclusion to your scene that makes a satisfactory ending?

- Do you learn a lesson? Do you make a decision?

- Do you come to an understanding?

PRE-WRITING LESSON: BROKEN NECKS AND BLANK MINDS

Objective: Students will begin to understand the importance of "painting a clear picture with words" for their readers.

Lesson set-up: A projector is required, as well as an assortment of interesting pictures. (Pictures that work best for this activity are simple yet interesting ones: a silhouette of a cat next to a broken glass or a dog dressed in a suit.) This lesson works best if your room has individual tables/desks, but can be adapted to any seating arrangement. Place blank sheets of paper and pencils on each table, and assign students into pairs. Tell them to face each other—one facing the front (Describers) and one facing the back wall (Drawers).

1. Tell your students "Your readers' minds are blank; they have no idea what your experience was. It is up to you to paint what happened well so they can experience it with you. Today we are going to mimic this experience through the use of some visuals."

2. Tell the students who are facing the back wall (Drawers): "You have broken necks and blank minds (You cannot turn around, and your mind is completely empty, like a clean slate).

3. Tell students who are facing the screen (Describers), "Your responsibility is to describe the picture on the screen to your partner so that he/she can draw it correctly. You, as "describers," are not allowed any hand motions—no pointing or gesturing—you may only use words."

4. Tell the (Drawers), "You may not ask questions—even for clarification –and you may not use hand gestures, either. Your job is to draw, according to the description that your partner provides."

5. When the Drawers are facing the back, project a picture on the screen for the Describers to see. Provide between 6-8 minutes for describing/drawing. Give warnings regarding how much time they have ("Two minutes left…") and when the time is up, tell the Drawers that they can turn around to see the actual picture. Have students sign their drawings (with both names) and turn them in. My students love to see each other's drawings under the overhead projector. After viewing (and laughing) at the pictures, discuss the experience of both sides. Tie the concept of writing to this activity: "Readers don't know anything about your lives. It is your responsibility to 'paint' your story so that they are engaged and have enough (but not too much) detail to become involved."

6. Have partners switch spots and then repeat the activity.

SCEDS Lesson Plans

SCEDS Lesson One: The Basics—Writing with Sensory Details

Objective: Students will write about a place using sensory details.

1. Give your students a setting and the sensory details observation chart.

   This lesson can be used in limitless situations. I have had them write about my classroom, about the hallway and about our school's courtyard on a nice day. It doesn't matter what setting you choose. This activity will help students gain confidence about their ability to write about any place—no matter how ordinary.

2. Allow students a fixed amount of time just to sit, observe and record details (at least ten minutes). The longer they focus on the sensory details around them, the better their writing will be.

3. When the time limit for observing is up, have them write a paragraph describing the setting.

   Because I usually take my students to a place outside of my classroom, the note-taking and writing activities are completely separate. When we return to the room, I have them write about the observed place for at least ten minutes and I suggest that they try to use at least three details from each column. They can use more or less or none from a column, depending on their own feeling. They should not be concerned with spelling or punctuation, just with words.

4. After at least ten minutes of silent writing, I ask for volunteers to read.

   Usually I have many volunteers, but if I don't, I offer extra credit and then they will read for sure.

5. Ask students to reflect on their writing.

   Since their paragraphs will sound like poetry, it is a good idea to have them reflect on what made their writing good so that the use of descriptive detail is affirmed.

   Julie's response - written from observations made in our school courtyard:

   As I sit on this rough old picnic table, I take in a deep breath and inhale the clean scent of Mathew's cologne. I feel cool gusts of wind glide across the inch of skin that is exposed from my shirt raising up my back. While looking at my surroundings, I notice the dry, brown grass, the cloudless blue sky, and the hot sun shining down on me. I feel warm and cozy. The loose hairs from my ponytail brush against the skin on my face and tickles me.

   Trent's response – written from the same place:

   As I sit on this picnic table, the hot sun beats against my face and the cold wind blows against me. The pine trees stand tall and proud as the leaves rustle in the wind. The hum of the generator and the sound of the plane flying above drown out the words of the people talking by the buses. There are spider webs in the corner of the green arches next to the tan brick wall. The grass is brown, and the leaves are falling slowly from the trees. It smells like fall and clean air. My papers fly off the table as a gust of wind flows through.

Name_____

SCEDS Lesson One —Writing with Sensory Details

Identifying Sensory Details (SCEDS)

1. Directions: Make a note of everything you experience with your five senses. Take note of how to describe what you see and the feel of the ground beneath you and the air around you:

sight	sound	taste/smell	touch

2. On another sheet of paper, write a paragraph describing the surroundings you observed using the above details.

SCEDS Lesson Two: Setting—Painting a Place with Words

Objective: Students will describe a setting using sensory details.

1. Project a picture of a setting. Settings that generate the best descriptions for me are pictures of "haunted" places: an abandoned amusement park, a haunted house, a road to nowhere or a deserted hospital. If possible, include sound to accompany the picture—a suspenseful, scary soundtrack for a haunted place, or the sound of a snowboarder hitting snow for a winter sport picture.

2. Ask the class to offer words to describe each sensory detail separately and tell them they must write down at least three words in each column.

   Example—haunted house, sound category: crunching of leaves, wind rustling the trees, squeaky steps leading to the house, a mouse scurrying across the path.

   Go slowly and wait for the class to offer at least five or six descriptive words before you move onto the next one. This part usually takes at least fifteen minutes.

3. Repeat 1 & 2 with another setting.

4. Ask students to write themselves into one of these scenes using the sensory details from the chart. Allow them at least ten minutes of silent writing time and suggest that they include details from each column.

5. Ask for volunteers to read.

6. Ask students to reflect on the strategies that made their descriptions come alive.

   Tristan's response – written after identifying sensory details in a picture of an abandoned amusement park:

   I walk into the amusement park and I see an old, rusty Ferris wheel. I feel scared because the Ferris wheel squeaks as the wind whistles through the dead trees. The cold air hits my face and it sends a chill down my spine. I take a deep breath and smell rusted metal and old, rotten food. I see a popcorn maker with empty bags sitting beside it. I can feel the broken concrete through my shoes as I run over and jump up on the platform. The rats run out from under the warped wood. I look through the broken fence and see a large piece of metal. I go over to get a closer look and realize that it's a piece of a rollercoaster seat. Another chill runs down my spine.

   Grace's response – written after identifying sensory details in a picture of a snowy field surrounded by pine trees at night:

   It's finally winter and I wake up at 4 am to look outside. I see that it has snowed a lot, so I decide to stay awake and celebrate the fact that nobody is up. I finally get to soak in and enjoy the quiet, perfectly laid out snow I see in my yard. I make a cup of coffee with French Vanilla creamer. I put a long trench coat on that covers my blue flannel pajama pants and my Deathnote t-shirt. I walk outside with my coffee and feel free inside when I see how the straight and sparkly snow lights up the darkness, but of course the coldness instantly hits my face. I hold my coffee tightly since it is the only warmth I have and walk out into the snow, feeling sad that I just ruined its perfection. I ignore it and take a sip of my sweet coffee. I feel the wetness soak into my socks and shoes and decide to ignore it, too. I love the smell of the wet pine trees, which are loaded with snow. This is the best time of the year.

MacKenzie's response – written after identifying sensory details in a picture of an old, abandoned castle on a hill surrounded by fog:

As I walk up the wet, crumbly stairs I slip and quickly grab onto whatever I can to keep myself from falling off the side of the mountain. Looking down I can't see anything except for thick, smoke-like fog and some confused birds trying to fly through. Their caws echo off the eroded brick building. I quickly run inside to escape the raindrops slapping the back of my neck and the smell of mildew and dust hits my nostrils. Even though the rotting floral furniture makes the room feel less empty, but the hairs on my arms stand up. "Someone's here with me," I think to myself as I hear a squeak from the hallway.

Kiana's response – written after identifying sensory details in a picture of a hammock sitting in the middle of clear blue water:

I lay in my hammock, floating above the crystal clear water. It's so clear and light blue it looks like someone filtered the whole ocean. I gaze at the sky and let my body hang – feeling the strings push into my skin - while I watch the birds soar around the sun and disappear. I feel the mist of the water as I look over and see a small island across the shore with one palm tree and a man cooking fish. Dark clouds are approaching, overtaking the fluffy white ones above me. When I smell the spices behind me, I know it's time to go in and eat.

Name_____

SCEDS Lesson Two—Writing with Sensory Details

SETTING: PAINTING A PLACE WITH WORDS (SCEDS)

1. Describe the setting in the picture using the sensory details chart below (try to brainstorm at least three descriptions for each column):

Visual	Auditory	Feel/Touch	Smell/Taste

2. Describe setting #2:

Visual	Auditory	Feel/Touch	Smell/Taste

3. On another sheet of paper, use the sensory details from your chart to write yourself into either setting #1 or setting #2. Use details from each column.

SCEDS Lesson Two (B): Blending Setting Descriptions into Narratives

Objective: Students will learn how to describe settings effectively within their narratives.

1. Read Eli Peterson's excerpt from "Repressed" or Kayla Kinnard's excerpt from "Sticks and Stones."

2. Instruct students to circle all of the sensory details used to describe the setting —all references to sight, sound, smell, taste and touch.

3. Clarify which words should be circled by marking the passages under a document camera.

4. Tell students to re-write these sections without using any of these details, which will strip them down to basic (boring) sentences.

5. Invite students to read their stripped-down versions of these excerpts out loud. Discuss the differences in the picture painted for the reader.

Name_____

SCEDS Lesson Two (B):

Blending Setting Descriptions into Narratives

Effective descriptions paint vivid pictures in our minds. In this activity, our goal is to take vivid writing and reduce it to dull writing by extracting the life (sensory details) out of it.

Directions:

Step One: Circle all of the sensory details used to describe the setting in the excerpts below—circle all references to sight, sound, smell, taste and touch.

Excerpt from

"Repressed"

by Eliaud Peterson (from *Behind Closed Doors: Stories from the Inside Out*)

Sitting at the end of the cold, hard bed I stare at the wall. I want to leave but the nurses' eyes are on my door. The familiar smell of acidic hospital disinfectant fills my nose and makes me choke. I shift in the giant paper napkin, goose bumps rising on my skin from the cool air pumped into the room. I feel naked anyway, because I was stripped of everything "potentially dangerous" when I was admitted. I pull on my gown and try to cover my legs, but I know they have seen them and I don't like that. I don't let anyone see my scars.

A short, chubby male nurse walks in and says, "Do you want something to eat, sweetie? You're looking thin. You need to keep your strength up."

I ignore him. *Don't call me "sweetie,"* I think. *I don't know you.* My mind drifts through the fog of my day as my chest stirs in rhythm with the heart monitor next to me.

Excerpt from

"Sticks and Stones"

by Kayla Kinnard (from *We Are Absolutely Not Okay*)

I hear glasses being thrown against the walls. The loud noise of my father's rage wakes me from my sleep. I am nine years old and it is the night of New Year's Eve. The clock reads 11:00 p.m. I rip the covers off my sweating body and walk to my bedroom door. My heart feels like it is going to rip out of my chest and I don't know if I feel anger or fear. My adrenaline is through the roof, but it takes a good ten minutes to convince myself to open the door. I hear my parents arguing, but I can't make out the words. I eventually turn the knob and walk out toward the living room. I can see the destruction that my father has caused. This is a daily occurrence in my house. The walls are dripping and stained with the remains of filled glass mugs that have been smashed against the walls. Glass lies in shards across the floor. I see my mother standing in the living room and my father standing in the kitchen. I don't really know what the fight is about, but I am sure it is unimportant. It always is.

Step Two: Re-write these passages without using **any** of the sensory details circled.

SCEDS Lesson Three: Character—Painting a Portrait with Words

Objective: Students will describe a character using sensory details.

1.   Project a picture of a "character" on your overhead screen (the more interesting the person is, the better).

2.   Ask the class to offer words to describe each sensory detail separately and tell them they must write down at least three words in each column.

   Example: sight –olive skin, grey hair, bowler's hat, wrinkles at the corner of the eyes.

   Go slowly and wait for the class to offer at least five or six descriptive words before you move onto the next column. This part usually takes at least ten minutes.

3.   Repeat 1-3 with a different character.

4.   On another sheet of paper, ask students to write themselves into a scene where they meet one of the characters they have just described. Allow at least ten minutes for silent writing and suggest that they include details from each column.

5.   After at least ten minutes of silent writing, I ask for volunteers to read their descriptions.

6.   Ask students to reflect on the strategies that made their descriptions come alive.

Kendra's response – written from the sensory details observed from a picture of an older, wrinkled man wearing a blue golf hat and smoking a cigar:

I hurried back to the restaurant since I forgot my bag there when I closed up. I put my key into the keyhole and turned it. When I opened the door, the smell of cigar smoke hit me. "That's weird," I thought. "No one has been in here for hours." I walked around the counter to retrieve my bag when something blue caught my eye – it was popping up from a booth in the far corner of the restaurant. I grabbed the pepper spray out of my bag and cautiously approached the booth. I stared directly into the blue filmy eyes of a man who appeared to be in his late sixties. I noticed the wrinkles around his mouth as he smiled at me, while smoke rose from his cigar. I wanted to ask him who he was, but my fear would not allow words to come out. He seemed to be a phantom, or some kind of hallucination.

Aaron's response – written from the sensory details observed from a picture of a fair-skinned, dark-haired girl with icy grey eyes:

Her smoky grey eyes, translucent skin and dark, short hair make her look like someone out of a fairy tale. As she walks by, a strong scent of cherry blossoms hits me. She's wearing a striped shirt, skirt and high heels, and her heels click against the pavement to the rhythm of her sway. She looks at me and I want to talk to her, but I can't. I see the lights of the street reflected in her eyes as she continues on.

Name_____

SCEDS Lesson Three—Writing with Sensory Details

CHARACTER: PAINTING A PORTRAIT WITH WORDS (SCEDS)

1. Describe the character in the picture using the sensory details chart below (try to brainstorm at least three descriptions for each column):

Visual What does this person look like? Describe clothing, approximate age and possible occupation.	**Auditory** How does this person talk? Any other noises associated with him/her?	**Kinesthetic** Describe body language, mannerisms and habits.	**Smell** What odors might you associate with this person?

2. Describe Character #2:

Visual What does this person look like? Describe clothing, approximate age and possible occupation.	**Auditory** How does this person talk? Any other noises associated with him/her?	**Kinesthetic** Describe body language, mannerisms and habits.	**Smell** What odors might you associate with this person?

3. On another sheet of paper, use the sensory details from your chart to write yourself into a scene with either character #1 or character #2. Use details from each column.

SCEDS Lesson Three (B): Blending Character Descriptions into Narratives

Objective: Students will learn how to describe characters effectively within their narratives.

1. Read directions for blending character descriptions into narratives.

2. Discuss the descriptions listed.

3. Instruct students to rewrite the basic narrative(s) by adding character descriptions.

4. Invite them to read their rewrites out loud to the class, and discuss the flow of the writing. Ask students if they are able to "see" the character with these additions.

5. Read the excerpts from both student stories.

Name_____

SCEDS Lesson Three (B):

Blending Character Descriptions into Narratives

It's a very delicate balance between adding "not enough" and "too much" description for characters in your scene. If he/she is a main character, then you will want to use more descriptors—less if the character is secondary, and maybe none if the character is mentioned only once. Refrain from making long lists of traits; instead, blend the descriptions into the narrative so that it flows naturally.

Using the two student examples below, rewrite the sections on another piece of paper and include the descriptions into the flow of the narrative.

1. Brinnon Hall, "Lost Respect"

   a. Brinnon's SCEDS character brainstorming to describe his dad:

   buzzed hair
   muscular
   biceps look like miniature boulders underneath his skin
   golden hazel eyes
   deep smile lines
   pockmarks all over his cheeks from years of popping pimples
   abs feel like rocks when he pulls me in for a hug

   b. Blend the above descriptions into the following narrative:

   After we get past the metal detectors of both steel doors controlled by the guards, we have to walk up to another guard who tells us where to sit while we wait for my dad to get strip searched before he finally walks out.
   I spot him from the line of prisoners as soon as he steps through the door. He checks in with the guard and then walks over to us. He sits down in the chair with the taped yellow stripe on it.
   "So, how have you been, B? What happened to your face?" he says, motioning to my black eye and bloody nose.

2. Jaycee Schrenk, "Stained"

   a. Jaycee's SCEDS character brainstorming to describe her mom:

   High-pitched voice
   Dark-washed blue jeans
   White flowing tank top, white flip flops to match
   Fingers full of diamond rings
   Coach bracelets, ruby red earrings
   Always kissed me on the forehead

   b. Blend the above descriptions into the following narrative:

   "Baby girl, you are my princess, so that means I am the queen. And your father? He's nothing more than a bank account," my mom said as she hopped out of our silver Saab. I watched her walk to the cash machine and return to the car with stacks of hundred dollar bills—money to take me summer clothes shopping.

Excerpt from

"Lost Respect"

by Brinnon Hall (from *Behind Closed Doors: Stories from the Inside Out*)

After we get past the metal detectors of both steel doors controlled by the guards, we have to walk up to another guard who tells us where to sit while we wait for my dad to get strip searched before he finally walks out.

I spot him from the line of prisoners as soon as he steps through the door. His hair is buzzed, like usual, and he is extremely muscular. His biceps look like miniature boulders underneath his skin. He has golden hazel eyes, deep smile lines, and deep pockmarks all over his cheeks from years of popping pimples.

He checks in with the guard and then walks over to us. His abs feel like rocks up against my stomach when he pulls me in for one of his bear hugs. He sits down in the chair with the taped yellow stripe on it.

"So, how have you been, B? What happened to your face?" he says, motioning to my black eye and bloody nose.

Excerpt from

"Stained"

by Jaycee Schrenk (from *Behind Closed Doors: Stories from the Inside Out*)

"Baby girl, you are my princess, so that means I am the queen. And your father? He's nothing more than a bank account," my mom said in her high-pitched voice as she hopped out of our silver Saab. I watched her walk to the cash machine in her dark-washed destroyed blue jeans and white flowing tank top with white flip-flops to match. I knew my mom was beautiful for her age; her style was plain, yet flashy. Her fingers were full of diamond rings, her wrists glinted with Coach bracelets, and ruby red earrings dangled off her ears. She returned to the car with stacks of hundred dollar bills—money to take me summer clothes shopping.

We ran up and down the mall from store to store, my hands holding multiple shopping bags. I felt as if my head was about to explode from the thrill of getting whatever my heart desired. I knew that most 6th graders in my class could never do this. I also knew that my mom had a bad problem with money and our monthly shopping trips were a secret between us. I always felt guilty but my dad rarely ever noticed.

As I placed my stacks of clothes on the Pac Sun counter, I shot a guilty glance at my mom to make sure it was OK to buy everything I wanted. But she reassured me with a kiss on my forehead and handed the cashier four hundred dollar bills.

SCEDS Lesson Four: Emotional/Physical Response

Objective: Students will learn how to describe the physical impact of emotions.

Note: It is especially important to emphasize the physical feeling (heart racing, nose twitching) rather than more emotional descriptions (When I felt fear I felt like I was never going to get to the other side.) It is also fun to compare physical responses between students. When feeling fear, some people's teeth chatter while others feel tingly all over.

1. Again, I project pictures to elicit the feeling of each emotion:

    Thrill/Adrenaline Rush: I project either the same rollercoaster picture from the dialogue lesson or a picture of a car that looks like it is traveling at a fast pace.

    Anger/Rage: I project a picture of two silhouettes facing each other, mouths open, their body language obviously aggressive.

    Fear/Anxiety: I project the same pictures from the dialogue lesson—either a dark, gloomy forest or a shadowy figure on a dark street.

    Sadness/Despair: I project a picture of a person sitting with head in hands in silhouette.

    Joy/Happiness: I project a picture of a person jumping for joy in silhouette or a picture of someone holding a puppy.

2. I go through each column slowly, asking students to volunteer how they experience each emotion physically. Usually, I have to direct students toward stating the physical feeling, rather than stating another emotion. This class brainstorming time will allow most students to come up with their own answers.

3. Ask students to write about a time they experienced one of these emotions using the physical details they have brainstormed in their charts. Allow them at least ten minutes of silent writing time.

4. Ask for volunteers to read scenes out loud.

5. Ask students to reflect on the strategies that made their descriptions come alive.

    Santino's response – written after identifying his physical reaction when he feels anger:

    I feel my heart beat faster as my body receives adrenaline. Blood rushes to my face as it gets warm. My hands are shaking out of control as my breathing gets really heavy. All I can think about is how I am going to hurt him. My body can't seem to stop moving.

    Martin's response – written after identifying his physical reaction when he feels the thrill of adrenaline:

    As I walk up the stairs to get on the Ring of Fire, my palms start to sweat. My heart is beating ten times faster than normal. I start to picture my seatbelt ripping off and me slipping off my seat and I feel like my insides are going to come out. There are over a thousand people around me, but all I can focus on are the noises of the rollercoaster's wheels. I'm getting so light-headed that I feel I can float away like a balloon filled with helium. "Martin! Hurry, it's almost our turn!" I look up and see a beautiful girl with amazing hair and bomb lips. I swear, every time I see her I melt. Then I remember, Oh, that's why I'm getting on this thing!

Destanee's response – written after identifying her physical reaction when she feels anger:

I'm sitting in my room looking at the folded up note from my father. My hands begin to scrunch into fists and I feel my fingernails dig into my sweaty palms. I open one hand to feel my face – it's beet red, so hot, like magma. I open the letter slowly and hair stands up on the back of my neck. When I swallow, it feels like a razor blade is scratching the back of my throat.

Name_____

SCEDS Lesson Four: Emotional/Physical Response

EMOTIONS: WRITING TO CONVEY THE PHYSICAL IMPACT OF EMOTIONS (SCEDS)

1. For each emotion listed, use concrete details to describe how the emotion feels to you physically:

Emotions:	What happens to your body physically when you feel this emotion?
Thrill/Adrenaline Rush	
Anger/Rage	
Fear/Anxiety	
Sadness/Despair	
Joy/Happiness	

2. On another sheet of paper, choose one scenario to describe. Use all elements of SCEDS, if possible, but especially focus on your emotions and how you experience them physically.

Name_____

SCEDS Lesson Four (B): Adding Emotional/Physical Response

Directions: Cross out all emotional/physical responses, and read the excerpts without them. Discuss the difference.

Excerpt from

"Loser, Failure, Dumbass"

by Maize Phillips (from *Behind Closed Doors: Stories from the Inside Out*)

"Hey guys, look! There's Maize! The class retard!" Kristopher Clayman screams out loud enough for me to hear two blocks away. The laughter surrounding him drowns him out for a moment. "Do you think he'll ever be smart enough to know that he might as well just die because he's so fucking worthless?"

Kris has been doing this for the entire school year. My hands are clenched into fists and I want to cover his face in scars. I want to destructively injure him, but leave him alive just so I can make him suffer more. I want to burn his skin off with my rage and break out his teeth with my fists. I am shaking with anger and I think I am going to lose control.

Excerpt from

"The Monster within Him"

by Marika Evenson (from *Behind Closed Doors: Stories from the Inside Out*)

The news anchor appears on the TV screen with the words "child rape arrest" and a picture of handcuffs above him. My stomach is in my throat.

"A man already convicted once of child rape is now suspected of raping another child, and KIRO7 reporter Amy Clancy has dug up the details. She's live downtown where the suspect just went before a court," he says. My hands are clammy as I rub them up and down on my tense, trembling knees.

The screen flashes to a wrinkled blonde woman. "Forty-two year old Jeffrey Evenson is a Level Three sex offender. According to these documents, he has raped again. His alleged victim—a then six-year-old girl," she says and my heart evaporates into thin air.

I see multiple mug shots of my father, and even though I'm disgusted to have the same last name as him, I'm thinking that the reporter could at least pronounce it correctly.

Then the real news begins.

"He was convicted in 1990 for child rape, in 1998 for child molestation and he was convicted twice for failing to register as a sex offender. On Tuesday, he was arrested again in Seattle for allegedly raping a now nine-year-old girl after the girl's father called police."

My ears turn off, my eyes blur and I feel a heavy pressure in my chest.

SCEDS Lesson Five: Dialogue—Bringing Scenes to Life with Dialogue, Blocking and Emotion

Objective: Students will learn how to add dialogue and emotional response to increase the action in their narrative scenes.

1. Project a picture that will elicit an emotional response in both scenarios:

   Scenario One: I project a picture of people on top of a rollercoaster with their hands in the air, ready to descend (on Google Images) on the overhead screen.

   Scenario Two: I project either a picture of a dark forest or a shadowy figure on a dark street.

   These pictures help to place students in the moment, experiencing the feeling and remembering times they have been in similar situations. If possible, include sound to accompany the pictures—a rollercoaster in motion or echoing footsteps.

   *If students have not ridden a rollercoaster, either ask for a similar scenario that might evoke an adrenaline rush, or allow them to fictionalize the experience of riding a rollercoaster. The rollercoaster scenario works well for most students.

2. I go through each column slowly and ask students to place themselves there, saying "Who might be with you on the rollercoaster? What is she saying? What are you saying? What is he doing while he is saying this? How do you feel?" and take a few suggestions to spur ideas for those who are slower to imagine the scenario. Students are instructed to fill in the chart or take notes as we brainstorm for each column.

3. Once the chart is complete, tell students to choose one scenario to write about, using all of the details they have brainstormed. Allow students to write silently for at least ten minutes.

4. Ask for volunteers to read scenes out loud.

5. Ask students to reflect on the strategies that made their descriptions come alive.

   Shelby's response, written after brainstorming dialogue from a picture of a rollercoaster:

   She stands at the front of the line, the wind carrying her fiery red hair; it flows back and forth around her face. You can tell she's nervous by the way her palms are sweating while she grips my hand, her grip getting tighter and tighter the closer we get to the rollercoaster.

   "Shelby, you know I'm scared of rollercoasters, I don't think I'm ready for this, do you see how far up it goes?" She bites her bottom lip and her face starts to get red.

   "Madison, you'll be fine, I know it's scary but I'll be here with you and you can even hold my hand if you want," I say to her. I love riding rollercoasters, the thrill of getting whipped around in a little cart, barely strapped in. My adrenaline starts running as we sit down in the little cart. The rollercoaster attendant comes to our cart dressed in a vest with the rollercoaster's name written in cursive.

   He speaks in a monotone voice and pops his gum as he gives instructions. Madison and I pull the bar down as close at it will get to our legs, the cold metal waking up the skin under the bar. The track starts clicking as we begin to climb the huge incline in front of us.

"Shelby this is so scary!" Madison screams. My stomach drops as we start down the incline; I let out a scream and throw my hands up in the air, my body getting thrown into the wall of the cart and then thrown into Madison's side.

"AHHHHH, WOOHOOO!" Madison and I both scream together. We go around a loop and they suspend us upside down. My face heats up while the other passengers scream. The rollercoaster makes us go flying backwards and we finally come to a stop, the bar now warm with how tight we are gripping it. It flies up and lets us free. I get up and my legs feel like Jell-O, but my grin widens as I help Madison stand up.

"We should go on the bigger one next!" she says excitedly.

Name_____

SCEDS Lesson Five: Dialogue—Bringing Scenes to Life with Dialogue, Blocking and Emotion

1. **DIALOGUE** (SCEDS): Add dialogue, blocking and emotional response to the following scenarios:

Scene	What is said?	Blocking: What are you and _____ doing while you are talking?	What is your emotional response?
You are on a roller coaster with your (best friend, brother, sister, aunt, grandmother, uncle, dad ...) _____: Name of person	You: _____:	You: _____:	
You and (your best friend, a bully, brother, sister, aunt, grandmother, uncle, dad. . .) are being chased by (?) _____: Name of person	You: _____:	You: _____:	

2. On another sheet of paper, choose one of these scenarios to write about using the dialogue, blocking and emotions identified in the chart.

SCEDS Lesson Five (B):   Bringing Scenes to Life with Dialogue, Blocking and Emotion

Objective: Students will learn the importance of using dialogue—rather than summary.

1. Read Emma Norton's excerpt from "Sick and Tired of Being Sick and Tired."

2. Read Emma's story again, this time without any dialogue, blocking or emotion. Discuss the difference.

3. Read Joey Reed's excerpt from "A Strife in My Life."

4. Instruct students to re-write this portion of Joey's narrative in the same way that Emma's has been stripped down: to remove all dialogue, blocking and emotion (turn it into summary).

5. Have students share their stripped-down versions. Discuss (and laugh).

Name_____

SCEDS Lesson Five (B): Bringing Scenes to Life with Dialogue, Blocking and Emotion.

Directions:

Step One: Read Emma's excerpt from "Sick and Tired of Being Sick and Tired."

Excerpt from

"Sick and Tired of Being Sick and Tired"

by Emma Norton (from Behind Closed Doors: Stories from the Inside Out)

A tall, thin cop approaches us. I can tell by his muscled arms that he's in good shape. He has a thick mustache and stubble on his jaw. He acknowledges us with that smartass look that cops have, like he's the coolest.

"You know, this is a no trespassing zone," he says.

Sam does the talking and I keep my mouth shut. "Oh, I'm sorry officer. We were just talking and didn't know it was a no trespassing zone." She tries to sound sweet while standing in front of the bong to hide it.

"Please sit down on the edge of the wall," the cop asks with a hint of a demand.

We hesitate for a minute but end up following his direction. He sees the bong shoved into the corner and points to it, giving us a knowing look.

"That was here when we got here," Sam says quickly. "It's not ours. We were just looking at it." I can tell he isn't buying it from his hard eyes staring at us.

"It really isn't ours. There's not even anything in it," Sam says, trying harder to convince him.

He takes it and gives us a look like he isn't stupid. "Okay, well, I'm going to throw it away in that dumpster," he says.

"Wait, can I do it?" Sam asks. I watch her walk to a big green dumpster and toss it in while I'm still sitting on the edge of the wall. I frown at the dumpster and forget about it.

Step Two: Now read Emma's excerpt without dialogue, blocking or emotional response:

A tall, thin cop approaches us. I can tell by his muscled arms that he's in good shape. He has a thick mustache and stubble on his jaw. He acknowledges us with that smartass look that cops have, like he's the coolest. He tells us it's a no trespassing zone and Sam tries to talk herself out of the situation but he tells us to sit down on the edge of the wall. He points to the bong and Sam claims it's not ours. He takes it and gives us a look like he isn't stupid and throws it in the dumpster, but Sam asks if she can do it herself.

.

Step Three: Read Joey's excerpt below:

Excerpt from

"A Strife in My Life"

by Joey Reed (from *You've Got it All Wrong*)

"What's in your backpack?" he asks.

They always ask me that. Every damn time.

"Um, papers and stuff," I answer.

"Do you have any sharpies in there?" he asks, motioning again to my backpack.

"No, my mom's too poor to get me one," I say, resting my hands on the back of my head.

"So, if I was to go up there and check, there won't be any graffiti on the walls up there then?" he asks, pointing his finger up to the roof.

Yeah, totally. I totally go up there where no one will be able to see anything and make a stupid gang tag that nobody will be able to read anyways. Totally.

"Uh, no. Besides, graffiti's something that all those stupid gangs do!" I state sarcastically.

"What's your name? he asks.

"Oh, it's Caleb," I reply.

He pulls a notepad and pen out of his chest pocket and begins to write something on it. "Okay, Caleb. What's your last name?"

I look up at him, trying to think.

"Uh, it's Caleb Reed," I say.

He wears a nametag, but I don't get to read it fully. I don't like it that he's rushing me; things never turn out well when I am rushed by people.

Step Three: Re-write Joey's excerpt by taking out all of the dialogue, blocking and emotional response.

SCENE CONSTRUCTION Lesson One: Flashbacks

Objective: Students will learn how to place a scene within a scene.

1. Reading scenes that use the flashback technique is a great way to familiarize students with this structure (excerpts from Brayan Hernandez' "Run Up or Shut Up" or Tattiyana Fernandez' "Replaced" are included). After reading the excerpts, I ask students to identify the transition sentences between present and past.

2. For practice: Tell students that they will be writing their own "Three-Paragraph Flashback" – a scene within a scene – and to focus specifically on smooth transitions.

3. Project a picture of an interesting setting. I use one of many pictures I have collected of "abandoned places" because they encourage a lot of imagination: an abandoned amusement park, a military island, a "road to nowhere," an empty house filled with sand.

4. Ask the class to offer words to describe each sensory detail separately and tell them they must write down at least three words in each column (just like they did for SCEDS lesson 2 on setting).

5. PRESENT: Have students write themselves into this setting using the sensory details they have just brainstormed.

6. PAST (FLASHBACK): For their second paragraph, they must transition into the story of how they arrived at this place. (These will get very creative – running from the law, "one wrong turn," a zombie apocalypse, etc.)

7. BACK TO THE PRESENT: For their last paragraph, they must transition their reader back to the present.

8. Ask for volunteers to read their scenes and to identify their transition sentences.

SCENE CONSTRUCTION Lesson One: Flashbacks

Excerpt from
"Run Up or Shut Up"
By Brayan Hernandez (from *We Are Absolutely Not Okay*)

"Don't be scared," my homeboy told me.

I was shaking. Sweat was building between the palm of my hand and the handle of the single action .22 revolver I was holding. I had never held a gun and, being the size that I was, I thought it was really heavy. I felt the pressure in my head, imagining how it could all go wrong. It seemed like the whole world knew what I was about to do and the glares of the few people that walked past terrified me. But I couldn't show any type of weakness. I had to make it seem like I was in control of the situation.

I had received the call that would place me here a couple of days before from one of my homeboys.

"What's good, little homie?" he had said over my cell phone's speakerphone. His ranking was a "Soldier," meaning he was one of many roots that held the gang in place. He had been in the click since it started.

"Nothing," I replied with a rough voice, trying to act tough.

"You down to put in work this weekend? Because there is a meeting set up and your cousin talked about you coming in. It's now or never little homie," he said in a voice that made my heart pump faster.

"Yeah," I mumbled, not wanting to hear or see what was coming next. "Is he going to be there?" I asked. My cousin had been in the gang for a couple months before I joined in and he was already ranked as "Third Word" in the gang, meaning that his words counted when the gang made a decision. We had moved from Mexico City two years earlier when I was ten. Neither of us had known anyone, and we couldn't speak to anyone. The transition was difficult, but through the gang we had found a family who understood what we were going through.

"Na, he says it's your decision and you're on your own. But don't worry. Ain't nothing out of the ordinary. We just going hunting, trying to get some cash. You up for it?" he asked.

"Alright then, I'm down" I said firmly. A feeling of desperation washed over me. I had just given my word and I couldn't let them down.

"Cool, I'll be seeing you little one," he said, and then hung up.

After that call my mind had just two thoughts, to rob or to leave and never step up. If I didn't do this I would never be able to join the gang.

A couple of days later, I was mobbing through the streets of downtown Everett with three other members and a gun, looking for a mark.

"All you got to do is point and ask for everything. If they don't give it up you just take it," one of my homeboys instructed me.

I didn't answer. I knew what I had to do. If it all went bad and the police found me or caught me in the act, I knew I had to keep my mouth shut.

Excerpt from
"Replaced"
By Tattiyanna Fernandez (from You've Got it All Wrong)

Here I stand in a room that I should recognize, but it's completely different. It's not my room. It's not the room that I painted, not the room I slept in just last week. I knew things were going to be different, and I knew I would have to share a room with the baby if it was a girl, which it was. But I didn't know they were going to completely change my room.

My light pink-colored walls, my twin-sized bed, my heart-patterned bed spread, my paintings and posters are all gone. The chandelier my dad put in especially for me, my clothes, my dresser…everything is gone. Just like that. It looks like a full on nursery. Baby clothes, baby toys and a crib. The walls are now purple with lady bugs and butterflies.

Where is all my stuff? Where's my bed? Where's all my art? Where do they expect me to sleep. With the dog? All these thoughts that are screaming and chanting in my head want to come out, but I won't let them. I know it's over. It's the day I know my dad is going to forget all about me.

I feel betrayed. Just weeks before, my step mom and I had a conversation on the phone.

"Hey, are you busy? I know you're getting ready to go camping with Payton but I wanted to ask you something," she said, all chipper-sounding, like usual.

"Alright what's up?" I replied. I was worried because whenever she started a conversation like that, it was something bad.

"Well if the baby is a girl, would it be okay if you guys shared a room? Being it's already girly and stuff?" she asked.

I breathed a sigh of relief.

"Yeah I'd be okay with that, as long and she doesn't cry too much! Ha-ha," I said, tying to joke around.

"Well, she wouldn't sleep there for a few months," she said.

"Oh, well, yeah, if it's a girl I'm totally fine with sharing my room," I said again, happy she had asked me first.

I had been completely fine with sharing my room with her. But when I see my changed room and all my stuff gone, it feels like there is a big rubber ball stuck in my throat. I want to cry, but I can't. Everything is blurry. I am looking at the new lady bug mini-ceiling fan through tears.

QUESTIONS FOR DISCUSSION

1. Where do the flashbacks begin and end?

2. What sentences transition the reader from present to past and back again?

Name_____

SCENE CONSTRUCTION Lesson One: Using Flashbacks to Sequence Events in a Scene

Definition:

flashback(n) - a scene in a story that is set in a time earlier than the main story.

Instructions: Write a three –paragraph scene in which you utilize the flashback technique (place a scene within a scene). You will move from present to past and back to present again. Your goal is to transition between them smoothly.

Paragraph One: PRESENT

Paragraph Two: PAST

Paragraph Three: BACK TO THE PRESENT

1. Describe the setting in the picture using the sensory details chart below (try to brainstorm at least three descriptions for each column):

Visual	Auditory	Feel/Touch	Smell/Taste

2. PRESENT: In your first paragraph, place yourself in this setting using these sensory details.

3. PAST (FLASHBACK): In your second paragraph, transition into the story of how you arrived at this place.

4. BACK TO THE PRESENT: In your last paragraph, transition back to the present.

SCENE CONSTRUCTION Lesson Two: Sequencing Events in a Scene

Objective: Students will learn how to sequence the events of a scene in order to include the past within the present moment.

1. Read directions for sequencing events in a scene worksheet, then have students read the events out loud for Brayan's scene.

2. Ask students to place events in an order that makes sense.

3. Go over their responses and discuss. Below is how Brayan Hernandez ordered the events in his scene "One Shot" (from You've Got it All Wrong):

__P___ a. ___He picks a fight in the gym with a Blood.

__FB _ b. ___He asks his cousin if he can join, cousin says he's too young.

__FB__ c. ___He asks the shot caller, who says he has to prove he is up for it.

__P____d. ___The fight is broken up and he gets escorted to the principal's office.

4. Repeat for the next three scenes. Answers may differ. The most important take-away from this lesson is that students consider how to place the reader in the moment while including important elements that have previously occurred.

SCENE CONSTRUCTION Lesson Two: Sequencing Events in a Scene

If the parts of a scene take place over a period longer than an hour (over the course of a day, a week or a month), events must be ordered using the flashback technique. Structuring events in this way will ground the story in a time and place and allow your reader to experience the moment with you.

Instructions: Consider the following story events and how you might order them using a flashback scene within the main (present) scene. Remember that the main scene must take place in a relatively short time period (usually under an hour).

Reorder the events in each scene. Place a "P" next to the events in the present, main scene and "FB" next to the events in the flashback.

1. Scene: Brayan wants to join a gang.

    a. He asks his cousin if he can join, cousin says he's too young.

    b. He asks the shot caller, who says he has to prove he is up for it.

    c. He picks a fight in the gym with a Blood.

    d. The fight is broken up and he gets escorted to the principal's office.

___ 1. _____

___ 2. _____

___ 3. _____

___ 4. _____

2. Scene: After Isabel's father disowns her, she tries to reconcile with him.

    a. Isabel's father sees her coming out of an apartment building with her boyfriend.

    b. Later that night he comes into her bedroom, whips her and tells her she is no longer his daughter.

    c. One month later, she tries to reconcile with him.

    d. Her father refuses her request.

___ 1. _____

___ 2. _____

___ 3. _____

___ 4. _____

3. Scene: Adam gets bullied to the breaking point.

    a. Adam gets bullied on the way to school every day by two boys.

    b. One day they decide to bully him during PE.

    c. He loses control, fights them and gets sent to the principal's office.

___ 1. _____

___ 2. _____

___ 3. _____

4. Scene: Tatti's room is redecorated for her new baby sister.

    a. Tatti's step mother asks her if she would mind sharing a room with her new baby sister. Tatti agrees.

    b. Weeks later, she sees the room and it's no longer hers. All of her stuff is gone and has been replaced with a crib and baby decorations.

    c. She asks her dad where she should sleep. He suggests the couch.

___ 1. _____

___ 2. _____

___ 3. _____

SCENE CONSTRUCTION Lesson Three: Engaging the Reader

The following excerpts come from *We Are Absolutely Not Okay*, *You've Got it All Wrong*, and *Behind Closed Doors: Stories from the Inside Out*.

Excerpt from "**A Taste of the Real World**" by Leandra Hall

"Oh come on, baby. I just wanna spend some time with you." The man's deep, low voice sent shivers down my spine. The feeling of his hand rubbing my upper back kept me frozen in fear. "How much will it take?"

Excerpt from "**Run Up or Shut Up**" by Brayan Hernandez

"Don't be scared," my homeboy told me.

I was shaking. Sweat was building between the palm of my hand and the handle of the single action .22 revolver I was holding.

Excerpt from "**Gone**" by Destiny Allison

My heart stopped when I heard my grandma speak the words. As if it wasn't bad enough hearing them the first time, they kept replaying in my head. "We went to your dad's house this morning. He's dead."

Excerpt from "**He Was My Hero**" by Isabel Cordova

It's been eight months since my dad and I have talked to each other. I am ready to confront him, tell him that I am sorry and ask him to forgive me.

Excerpt from "**Good Intentions, Bad Results**" by Shelby Asbury

"When we walk up those stairs, he's going to be there," the prosecutor says as we make our way toward the courtroom.

Excerpt from "**Repressed**" by Eli Peterson

Sitting at the end of the cold, hard bed I stare at the wall. I want to leave but the nurses' eyes are on my door.

1.   How does each lead engage you into the action of the scene?

2.   How does each lead orient you to the conflict of the story?

SCENE CONSTRUCTION Lesson Three: Engaging the Reader

Objective: Students will learn to engage readers into their stories by presenting the conflict within the first few sentences.

1. Ask students what draws them into a story. What makes them want to read more? How long do they "stick" with a story until they give up on it?

2. Read examples of good leads and ask students what makes each one compelling. Are the leads active? Do they state the conflict clearly?

3. After determining the qualities of a good lead, have them work in pairs to write leads for the examples given.

4. After ten minutes, ask students to share their leads.

5. Discuss each lead. Is it active? Is the conflict clear?

SCENE CONSTRUCTION Lesson Three: Engaging the Reader

To engage your reader from the very first sentence of your story, follow these two simple rules:

1. Begin with action.

2. Make the conflict clear.

Directions: Write a compelling lead for each scene below.

1. You are followed by three bullies on the way home from school. They are picking on you.

_____

_____

_____

_____

2. Police arrive at your house and handcuff you (or someone in your family).

_____

_____

_____

_____

3. You are driving on the freeway without a license and you see flashing lights behind you. You and your friends have been drinking.

_____

_____

_____

_____

Name_____

Writing with Sensory Details—Your Narrative Scene

SETTING: PAINTING A PLACE WITH WORDS (SCEDS)

1. Choose the real-time setting (usually the first setting) from your narrative scene.

2. Describe this setting using the sensory details chart below (try to brainstorm at least three descriptions for each column).

Visual	Auditory	Feel/Touch	Smell/Taste

3. Use this chart to brainstorm your secondary setting – it may be set within a flashback or another place you move to in real-time.

Visual	Auditory	Feel/Touch	Smell/Taste

4. On another sheet of paper, write a paragraph describing your first setting, then return to your second chart when you get to your next one.

Name_____

Writing with Sensory Details—Your Narrative Scene

CHARACTER: PAINTING A PORTRAIT WITH WORDS (SCEDS)

1. Choose a main character from your narrative scene:_____

2. Describe this person using the sensory details chart below (try to brainstorm at least three descriptions for each column).

Visual What does this person look like? Describe clothing, approximate age and possible occupation.	Auditory How does this person talk? Any other noises associated with him/her?	Kinesthetic Describe body language, mannerisms and habits.	Smell What odors might you associate with this person?

3. What is important for the reader to know about this character's background?

4. On another sheet of paper, write a paragraph describing this person using the above details plus an important fact from the background story.

Name_____

Writing with Sensory Details—Your Narrative Scene

EMOTIONS: WRITING TO CONVEY THE PHYSICAL IMPACT OF EMOTIONS (SCEDS)

1. Identify three emotions experienced during your narrative scene and describe how these emotions feel to you physically:

Event in your narrative scene:	Emotion experienced:	What happened to your body physically when you felt this emotion?

2. On another sheet of paper, choose at least one part of your narrative scene and describe your emotional/physical response to the events that happen.

Name_____

Writing with Sensory Details—Your Narrative Scene

DIALOGUE & EMOTIONAL RESPONSE (SCEDS)

1. Choose two events within your narrative and identify dialogue, blocking and your emotional response:

Event	What is said?	Blocking: What are you and _____ doing while you are talking?	What is your emotional response?
	You: _____:	You: _____:	
	You: _____:	You: _____:	

2. On another sheet of paper, choose one of these events to write about using the dialogue, blocking and emotions identified in the chart.

HIPPIE BOY TEACHING GUIDE

Vocabulary

Chapter 1

external conflict (n) – a struggle that occurs between a character and outside forces.

internal conflict (n) – a mental or emotional struggle that occurs within a character.

kinesthesia (n) – The sense that detects bodily position, weight, or movement of the muscles, tendons, and joints

gloat (v) – To express great, often malicious, pleasure or self-satisfaction

incredulous (adj) – Skeptical; disbelieving

venture (v)– An undertaking that is dangerous, daring, or of uncertain outcome.

smug (adj) – Feeling great or offensive satisfaction with oneself or with one's situation

Chapter 2

escalate (v) – To increase, enlarge, or intensify

celestial (adj) – Of or relating to the sky or the heavens

tuberculosis (n) – An infectious disease characterized by the coughing up of mucus, fever, weight loss, and chest pain.

confidante (n)– A woman to whom secrets or private matters are disclosed.

engross (v) – To occupy exclusively; absorb

Chapters 3 and 4

excommunication(n) – A formal disapproval by church leaders that deprives a person of the right to belong to a church.

adultery (n) – Voluntary sexual intercourse between a married person and a partner other than the lawful spouse.

reconcile (v) – To bring (oneself) to accept

Chapters 5 and 6

blocking (n) – a theater term that refers to the precise movement and positioning of actors on a stage in order to facilitate a performance.

excursion (n) – A short journey made for pleasure; an outing.

mortify (v) – To cause to experience shame, humiliation, or wounded pride; humiliate.

tourniquet (n) – A device, typically a tightly encircling bandage, used to check bleeding by temporarily stopping the flow of blood through a large artery in a limb.

accumulate (v) – To gather or pile up; amass.

Chapters 7, 8 and 9

implore (v) – to beg for urgently

condescending (adj) – displaying a patronizingly superior attitude

defiance (n) – bold resistance to an opposing force or authority

mesmerize (v) – to spellbind; enthrall

Chapters 10 and 11

accentuate (v) – make more noticeable or prominent

perforated (adj) – having a hole or holes, especially a row of small holes.

boomtown (n) – a town that experiences a sudden growth in business and population.

consignment (n)– goods shipped to a dealer who pays only for what is sold and who may return what is unsold.

story arc (n) – The purpose of a story arc is to move a character from one state to another; to effect change. This change or transformation often occurs when a character goes from a situation of weakness to one of strength.

Chapters 12 and 13

dilemma (n) – A situation that requires a choice between options that are equally unfavorable.

summon (v) – To request to appear; send for.

harrowing (adj) – Extremely distressing; agonizing.

desolate (adj) – Barren; lifeless.

savvy (adj) – knowledgeable about the realities of life.

rising action (n) – The events of a narrative plot that lead up to the climax (where the character goes through a transformation).

Chapters 14 and 15

foreshadow (v) – to show, indicate, or suggest in advance

climax (n) –The turning point in a plot or dramatic action. Where the character changes and begins to solve the conflict.

tirade (n) – A long angry or violent speech.

adjacent (adj) – Next to; adjoining.

extradite (v) – To give up or deliver (a fugitive, for example) to the legal jurisdiction of another government or authority.

embezzle (v) – To take (money, for example) for one's own use in violation of a trust.

Chapters 16, 17 and 18

falling action (v) – after the character changes during the climax, the events that take place to tie up the loose ends and bring the narrative story to a close is the falling action in the storyline.

resolution (n) –when the conflict has been resolved and the story has a finished, hopeful feel.

Name_____

Vocabulary

Chapter 1

external conflict (n) –

internal conflict (n) –

kinesthesia (n) –

gloat (v) –

incredulous (adj) –

venture (v)–

smug (adj) –

Chapter 2

escalate (v) –

celestial (adj) –

tuberculosis (n) –

confidante (n)–

engross (v) –

Chapters 3 and 4

excommunication(n) –

adultery (n) –

reconcile (v) –

Chapters 5 and 6

blocking (n) –

excursion (n) –

mortify (v) –

tourniquet (n) –

accumulate (v) –

Chapters 7, 8 and 9

implore (v) –

condescending (adj) –

defiance (n) –

mesmerize (v) –

Chapters 10 and 11

accentuate (v) –

perforated (adj) –

boomtown (n) –

consignment (n)–

story arc (n) –

Chapters 12 and 13

dilemma (n) –

summon (v) –

harrowing (adj) –

desolate (adj) –

savvy (adj) –

rising action (n) –

Chapters 14 and 15

foreshadow (v) –

climax (n) –

tirade (n) –

adjacent (adj) –

extradite (v) –

embezzle (v) –

Chapters 16, 17 and 18

falling action (v) –

resolution (n) –

Chapter 1 Teacher's Guide

Hippie Boy Chapter 1: (Pages 1-12)

SCEDS FOCUS: CHARACTER description and EMOTIONAL/physical response

Vocabulary:

- external conflict (n)—*A struggle that occurs between a character and outside forces.*

- internal conflict (n)—*A mental or emotional struggle that occurs within a character.*

- kinesthesia (n)—*The sense that detects bodily position, weight, or movement of the muscles, tendons, and joints.*

- gloat (v)—*To express great, often malicious, pleasure or self-satisfaction.*

- incredulous (adj)—*Skeptical; disbelieving.*

- venture (v)—*An undertaking that is dangerous, daring, or of uncertain outcome.*

- smug (adj)—*Feeling great or offensive satisfaction with oneself or with one's situation.*

1. Find the following sensory details used to paint a picture of the CHARACTER (SCEDS) Earl:

Visual What does Earl look like? What is he wearing?	**Auditory** What tone of voice does Earl use?	**Kinesthetic** What is his body language? What are his facial expressions?	**Smell** What odor surrounds Earl?
Snow clings to his greasy black hair like dandruff He's thick, short, 5'7" He has pasty white skin and a bulging gut He wears a plaid shirt and a giant silver belt buckle His eyes are icy blue and hard; they are magnified by thick glasses He has grease-stained, stubby fingers Later: he wears a navy blue mechanic jumpsuit with "Earl" embroidered on the pocket	*He gloats and speaks smugly when he feels powerful*	*He grips mom's hand tightly A small, mean smile creeps across his face when he feels powerful His eyes also dance when he feels powerful*	*He smells like rotting hamburger meat*

2. A character's background is also important for the reader to understand the whole picture. What is Earl's background?

He is a homeless Vietnam Vet who lives in a Chinook mini-camper. He's been divorced at least twice and has three or four children from other marriages. He's Mormon, but doesn't hold the highest priesthood given to worthy Mormon men.

3. For the event listed below, describe Ingrid's **EMOTIONAL** (SCEDS) and physical response as she feels that emotion.

Event	Emotional response	Physical response
Ingrid is waiting to hear Earl's decision about whether or not she can go with her dad	*Anger, powerlessness, anxiety*	*Her stomach feels like a hundred bees are buzzing inside of it, stinging her. Her hands tremble.*

4. Identify Ingrid's external and internal conflicts:

   External conflict: *She has power struggle with Earl and her mom is on Earl's side.*

   Internal conflict: *She needs to find the strength to stand up for herself.*

5. **SCENE CONSTRUCTION**: Consider the following elements to identify the STORY ARC— what does Ingrid learn through the events of this scene?

   Scene, pages 5-12: Earl Says "No"

   Scene opening: Dad drops by for an unexpected visit. It's the first time that he and Earl meet.

Component	
How does the scene opening set the stage for what is to come?	*The reader knows that things will not go smoothly between Earl and Ingrid's dad based on the little that has been revealed.*
What is the conflict?	*Ingrid can't stand Earl already, and he is given the power to decide if she can go with her dad to New Mexico for the weekend.*
How is this scene grounded in time and place? (What is the setting?)	*The scene is set in Logan, Utah at Ingrid's house.*
What is the context of this scene? What paragraphs add necessary background information for the present action to make sense? Are there any flashbacks?	*One paragraph explains that Ingrid has already told her dad about Earl, one explains how her parents used to get along, and one that describes her dad as an independent salesman who can't stand to be caged. The reader is also told why her siblings don't want to go with him.*

What action moves this scene along?	*Dad enters the house and is shocked over meeting Earl. He asks the kids if any of them want to come to New Mexico with him for the weekend. Only Ingrid wants to go. When she asks her mother, her mother defers to Earl. Earl answers that they must pray about it, and Ingrid must go between the two parties to get her answer.*
How does the scene end?	*Earl tells Ingrid that the Lord does not want her to go with her dad.*
What has been learned by Ingrid through the events of this scene?	*Ingrid decides that this is the last time Earl and her mother keep her from being with her dad.*

Artistic response to Chapter 1:

Draw a character anatomy of Earl using the sensory details you identified. Label at least five details with words taken from the pages of the book. Draw one speaking bubble and include something Earl said in the chapter.

Student Example:

Name_____

Chapter 1

Hippie Boy: (pages 1-12)

SCEDS FOCUS: CHARACTER description and EMOTIONAL/physical response

1. Find the following sensory details used to paint a picture of the **CHARACTER** (SCEDS) Earl:

Visual What does Earl look like? What is he wearing?	**Auditory** What tone of voice does Earl use?	**Kinesthetic** What is his body language? What are his facial expressions?	**Smell** What odor surrounds Earl?

2. A character's background is also important for the reader to understand the whole picture. What is Earl's background?

3. For the event listed below, describe Ingrid's **EMOTIONAL** (SCEDS) and physical response as she feels that emotion.

Event	Emotional response	Physical response
Ingrid is waiting to hear Earl's decision about whether or not she can go with her dad		

4. Identify Ingrid's external and internal conflicts:

External conflict:

Internal conflict:

5. SCENE CONSTRUCTION: Consider the following elements to identify the STORY ARC—what does Ingrid learn through the events of this scene?

Scene, pages 5-12: Earl Says "No"

Scene opening: Dad drops by for an unexpected visit. It's the first time that he and Earl meet.

Component	
How does the scene opening set the stage for what is to come?	
What is the conflict?	
How is this scene grounded in time and place? (What is the setting?)	
What is the context of this scene? What paragraphs add necessary background information for the present action to make sense? Are there any flashbacks?	
What action moves this scene along?	
How does the scene end?	
What has been learned by Ingrid through the events of this scene?	

QUESTIONS FOR DISCUSSION/WRITING

a.   How do you feel about Ingrid's mother after this chapter?

b.   How does the first sentence of the book pull you into the story?

c.   Ingrid's need to escape is clear by the end of the first chapter. In what ways have you tried to escape your life?

d.   When did you vow to "never again" let something happen to you?

e.   Earl makes a very important decision for Ingrid. When have you been treated unjustly by an authority figure and how did that make you feel?

f.   How have someone else's religious beliefs been forced on you?

HIPPIE BOY SMALL SKETCH

Chapter One: Earl Says "No" (Ingrid, Mom, Dad, Earl)

Ingrid: Mom, can I go with Dad for the weekend?

Mom: You'll have to ask Earl.

Ingrid (seething as she turns to face Earl, speaking through clenched teeth): Can I go with my dad to New Mexico for the weekend?

Earl (gloating): I don't know. Your mother and I are going to have to pray about it.

Ingrid (to mom, desperate): Mom, can I please go with Dad? He's waiting for me.

Mom: We're going to have to pray about it.

(Earl and Mom walk down the hall. Ingrid is incredulous. They return.)

Earl (to Ingrid, smugly): What about church? You have to go to church.

Ingrid (goes back to Dad): Dad, they say I have to go to church. Is there a way we can find a church in New Mexico?

Dad: Tell them whatever the hell they want to hear!

Ingrid (to Mom): Dad says they will make sure that I attend church.

Earl: Your mother and I will have to pray about it some more.

(Ingrid holds back screams as they go back down the hall)

Ingrid (holding her breath): Well?

Earl: Ingrid, I'm sorry, but the answer is "no." The Lord doesn't want you to go with your dad at this time.

Ingrid (to mom, begging between sobs): Mom, please let me go! This is important to me!

Mom (avoiding eye contact with Ingrid): You heard what Earl said. The answer is "no."

Chapter 2 Teacher's Guide

Hippie Boy (pages 13-42)

SCEDS FOCUS: CHARACTER BACKSTORY and CHARACTER DESCRIPTION

Vocabulary:

escalate (v)—*To increase, enlarge, or intensify.*

celestial (adj)—*Of or relating to the sky or the heavens.*

tuberculosis (n)—*An infectious disease characterized by the coughing up of mucus, fever, weight loss, and chest pain.*

confidante (n)—*A woman to whom secrets or private matters are disclosed.*

engross (v)—*To occupy exclusively; absorb.*

1. What decision does Ingrid's mother make for the family and how does Ingrid feel about this news?

   She yanks them out of school and moves them to Mississippi. Ingrid is thrilled to be with her dad.

2. What are Mormon fathers "supposed" to be like, according to Ingrid's mom?

   Fathers are supposed to be at home, watching over their children and guiding them with priesthood powers.

3. **CHARACTER DESCRIPTION** (SCEDS): Identify the following sensory details used to describe Ingrid's dad:

Visual What does he look like? What does he wear?	Auditory What tone of voice does he use?	Kinesthetic What is his body language? What are his facial expressions?	Smell
He's as handsome as a movie star with strawberry blonde hair like Elvis' *He has big, warm hazel eyes.* *He dresses nicely, in either a suit or jeans and a button-down shirt. He wears real cowboy boots.*	*He has a loud, booming voice that makes people listen.* *He has a golden tongue—he can talk his way out of anything.*	*When he smiles his whole face lights up.*	—

4. Find the following sensory details used to describe Ingrid's mom:

Visual What does she look like? What does she wear?	**Auditory** What tone of voice does she use?	**Kinesthetic** What is her body language? What are her facial expressions?	**Smell**
She dresses in frumpy clothes from the church thrift store	*She speaks with a meek, quiet voice in a thick Austrian accent.*	*She rarely smiles.*	*(Avon perfume mentioned in chapter one)*

5. Instead of TELLING you about her weekend fantasy ("I imagined all the fun things we would do at the Holiday Inn"), list at least four details she uses to SHOW what she is imagining:

   a. *They would get a top-floor room with a view.*

   b. *They would order room service.*

   c. *They would watch TV with a remote control while leaning on a pile of pillows.*

   d. *They would sleep in, watch cartoons and order pancakes with whipped cream for breakfast.*

6. How does the weekend actually turn out?

   She ends up sleeping on the floor at Patricia's apartment while her dad cheats on her mother with Patricia.

7. **CHARACTER BACKSTORY** (SCEDS): Mom's story

   a. Why did Ingrid's mother's stepmother hate her?

   Because her stepmother's husband had an affair with another woman, and Ingrid's mom was the product of that affair.

   b. What happened to her real mom?

   She was captured by the Nazis while working for the Resistance Movement.

   c. What things did her stepmother do to her?

   When she was drunk she would lock her in a room and threaten to kill her with a knife, make her sell her doll, force her to beg for liquor.

   d. What happened at the bomb shelter?

   An entire family hiding with them died during an explosion. She came out to find dead bodies and their apartment in rubble.

   e. What sealed her mother's decision to convert to Mormonism at age 16?

   She heard a voice quoting a scripture from the Book of Mormon after praying for an answer.

f. At the end of the chapter, what does Patricia give to Ingrid and what happens as a result of that gift?

Patricia gives Ingrid a calculator and when Ingrid's mother finds out the details of the night, she moves her family back to Utah.

Name_____

Chapter 2 Pre-reading

1. **CHARACTER BACKSTORY** (SCEDS):

    Use at least seven of the following words to create a fictional backstory for Ingrid's mother (you are about to learn the true story):

    Austria

    1940

    police officer

    stepmother

    bad

    ugly

    disgrace

    poor

    teased

    begged

    taverns

    sell

    doll

    struggled

    window

    play

    sick

    explosion

    bomb

    rubble

    dead

Name_____

Chapter 2

Hippie Boy: (pages 13-42)

SCEDS FOCUS: CHARACTER BACKSTORY and CHARACTER DESCRIPTION

1. What decision does Ingrid's mother make for the family and how does Ingrid feel about this news?

2. What are Mormon fathers "supposed" to be like, according to Ingrid's mom?

3. **CHARACTER DESCRIPTION** (SCEDS): Identify the following sensory details used to describe Ingrid's dad:

Visual What does he look like? What does he wear?	Auditory What tone of voice does he use?	Kinesthetic What is his body language? What are his facial expressions?	Smell

4. Find the following sensory details used to describe Ingrid's mom:

Visual What does she look like? What does she wear?	Auditory What tone of voice does she use?	Kinesthetic What is her body language? What are her facial expressions?	Smell

5. Instead of TELLING you about her weekend fantasy ("I imagined all the fun things we would do at the Holiday Inn"), list at least four details she uses to SHOW what she is imagining:

    a.

    b.

    c.

    d.

6. How does the weekend actually turn out?

7. CHARACTER BACKSTORY (SCEDS): Mom's story

    a. Why did Ingrid's mother's stepmother hate her?

    b. What happened to her real mom?

    c. What things did her stepmother do to her?

    d. What happened at the bomb shelter?

    e. What sealed her mother's decision to convert to Mormonism at age 16?

8. At the end of the chapter, what does Patricia give to Ingrid and what happens as a result of that gift?

QUESTIONS FOR DISCUSSION/WRITING

1. Discuss Ingrid's mother. How do you think her childhood shaped her decisions as an adult and her need to be guided by religion? Are you more sympathetic towards her after reading about her childhood?

2. When did hearing someone's story change the way you viewed him/her?

3. Why do you think Ingrid so readily identified with her dad and was willing to forgive his faults and shortcomings? Is there someone similar in your life?

4. Regarding Ingrid's dream weekend/nightmare reality: When have you been promised something that was not delivered? What did that disappointment feel like?

5. After the calculator incident, Ingrid believes that it is her fault when her mom leaves her dad and moves them back to Utah. When have you blamed yourself for something that was out of your control?

6. How does the failed trip to Mississippi serve as a foreshadowing for the rest of the book?

7. How is flashback used in this chapter? How does the flashback deepen your understanding of Ingrid's relationship with her dad?

HIPPIE BOY SMALL SKETCH

Chapter Two: Ingrid's Fantasy Crushed (Ingrid, Dad, Patricia)

Dad: Well, there you are, Ingrid. Guess what? Patricia just offered to let us spend the night here. Wasn't that nice of her?

Ingrid (feeling like she's been punched in the stomach): But Dad, I thought we were going to get a room at the Holiday Inn.

Dad: I know, but it's late and it'll be hard to find a motel room. Plus, we'll save money.

Ingrid: But what about room service?

Dad: It's probably closed by now, anyway.

(Dad leads her to the hallway, Patricia gives her a pillow and a blanket): This is just fine, isn't it, Ingrid?

(Ingrid bites her lip to hold back tears and nods her head.)

Patricia: Are you sure you're doing to be okay out here?

Ingrid nods again, but as soon as they leave, she lets the tears come.

Chapters 3 & 4 Teacher's Guide

Hippie Boy: (pages 43-62)

SCEDS FOCUS: SETTING/SCENE DESCRIPTION

Vocabulary:

excommunication(n)—*A formal disapproval by church leaders that deprives a person of the right to belong to a church.*

adultery (n)—*Voluntary sexual intercourse between a married person and a partner other than the lawful spouse.*

reconcile (v)—*To bring (oneself) to accept.*

Chapter 3

1. Ingrid thinks her dad is mad at her for telling about the calculator. What is really going on?

    Her dad is being ex-communicated from the church for having an affair.

2. **SETTING DESCRIPTION** (SCEDS): Ingrid TELLS us that their "depressing, run-down state of our house" affected her and then provides us with sensory details to SHOW what made it so:

Visual	Auditory	Touch/Feel	Smell/Taste
Dirty greyish "white" walls with crumbling plaster Mismatched kitchen rugs cover the flowered carpet in the living room Water-damaged black chairs A giant aluminum trash can that holds powdered milk A washing machine is used for counter space and a cutting board	*Flies swarm around the kitchen*	———	*A laundry hamper smells up the kitchen Sticky dead flies fall from the fly strip above the table into their food*

3. **SETTING/SCENE DESCRIPTION** (SCEDS): The scene where Ingrid jumps out of a "cake" to surprise her dad comes to life through the use of sensory details. Identify them in the chart below:

Visual	Auditory	Touch/Feel	Smell/Taste
Her revealing outfit: strawberry-patterned terry cloth shorts and a halter top, mascara *The box stuffed with newspaper strips*	*She ignores her growling stomach.*	*The box is just big enough for her to sit with her knees pulled to her chest.* *Sweat rolls down her back and she can feel the newspaper strips sticking to her legs.* *Her hair is matted against her face.*	*The air in the box turns hot and clammy.* *The neighbors are eating Sloppy Joes, potato chips and orange soda while she waits in the box.*

Chapter 4

1. Name a few things that Ingrid's dad destroyed during fights with her mom:

    He smashes their TV, part of a wall, their "new chandelier" and the piano bench.

2. Instead of TELLING you about her Osmond Family Rescue fantasy ("I imagined being rescued from my life by the Osmond family."), list five details she uses to SHOW what she is imagining:

    a. *There had been a mix-up at the nursery and the Osmonds had secretly been looking for her for years.*

    b. *She would be rescued and driven by stretch limo to the Osmond compound.*

    c. *She would enter Donny's purple room through a long tunnel and sit on his purple-quilted bed.*

    d. *Donny would tell her he wouldn't let anyone hurt her again.*

    e. *The whole family would have a feast for her and then show her to her new room.*

Name_____

Chapters 3 & 4

Hippie Boy: (pages 43-62)

SCEDS FOCUS: SETTING/SCENE DESCRIPTION

Chapter 3

1. Ingrid thinks her dad is mad at her for telling about the calculator. What is really going on?

2. **SETTING DESCRIPTION** (SCEDS): Ingrid TELLS us that their "depressing, run-down state of our house" affected her and then provides us with sensory details to SHOW what made it so:

Visual	Auditory	Feel/Touch	Smell/Taste

3. **SETTING/SCENE DESCRIPTION** (SCEDS): The scene where Ingrid jumps out of a "cake" to surprise her dad comes to life through the use of sensory details. Identify them in the chart below:

Visual	Auditory	Feel/Touch	Smell/Taste

Chapter 4

1. Name a few things that Ingrid's dad destroyed during fights with her mom:

2. Instead of TELLING you about her Osmond Family Rescue fantasy ("I imagined being rescued from my life by the Osmond family."), list five details she uses to SHOW what she is imagining:

    a.

    b.

    c.

    d.

    e.

QUESTIONS FOR DISCUSSION/WRITING

1. Discuss Ingrid's home life and how it affected her social life. Were you ever embarrassed about your house or your family to the point that you didn't want to invite your friends over?

2. Why did Ingrid go to such great (and embarrassing) lengths to get attention from her dad? What lengths have you gone to for the sake of getting attention?

3. What part of Ingrid's escape fantasy was believable? What is your rescue or escape fantasy?

Hippie Boy Small Sketch

Chapter Three, Scene One: Ingrid Jumps out of a "Cake"

(Ingrid, Dad, Mom, Heidi)

Ingrid (to Heidi): What I want you to do is wrap me in a box with the cake, and then I'll jump out and surprise him.

(Heidi helps Ingrid cut up the Sunday paper and stuffs it in the box. Ingrid is inside with her knees pulled to her chest.)

Ingrid (to Heidi): Hurry up! He's going to be here any minute!

Ingrid (to Heidi): Heidi, I can't breathe! You've got to get me some air!

(Heidi runs to get scissors and punches holes in the box.)

Mom (after an hour has gone by): Ingrid, we're going to the neighborhood block party to eat Sloppy Joes.

Ingrid: OK, I will be over as soon as Dad gets home!

Heidi (after another long time of waiting, when Dad finally arrives): Hi, Dad. Open your present.

Ingrid (jumping out of the box): Surprise!

Dad: Well, this is nice. **(He goes to the kitchen, Ingrid is crushed.)**

CHAPTERS 5 & 6 TEACHER'S GUIDE

Hippie Boy: (pages 63-86)

SCEDS FOCUS: DIALOGUE

Vocabulary:

blocking (n)—*A theater term that refers to the precise movement and positioning of actors on a stage in order to facilitate a performance.*

excursion (n)—*A short journey made for pleasure; an outing.*

mortify (v)—*To cause to experience shame, humiliation, or wounded pride; humiliate.*

tourniquet (n)—*A device, typically a tightly encircling bandage, used to check bleeding by temporarily stopping the flow of blood through a large artery in a limb.*

accumulate (v)—*To gather or pile up; amass.*

Chapter 5

1. **DIALOGUE** (SCEDS) Identify the actions and emotional responses described with the dialogue during the grocery shopping scene:

Event	What is said?	Blocking: What are the characters doing while they are talking?	What is the emotional response?
Dad wants Ingrid and Connie to go grocery shopping. (page 63)	Dad: "Go get your shoes on. You two are doing the grocery shopping."	*He is pacing next to the table and looks like a lion ready to pounce.*	*Ingrid and Connie are fearful yet relieved that he doesn't seem to be mad at them.*
Mom responds to dad's demand. (page 64)	Mom: "Jerry, you can't let them do the grocery shopping. That money has to last us the entire month."	*Her lower lip quivers.*	*They can't look at Mom because they feel caught in between.*
Connie and Ingrid are at the Wonder Bread Outlet. (page 69)	Connie: "Look, Ingrid, ten loaves for one dollar. Mom is going to LOVE this."	*She motions to the sign by the bread.*	*They both feel satisfied, like they have done a good job.*
They return home with the groceries.	Dad: "Well, look at this. It looks like you girls did just fine. I knew you would."	*He eyes the two carts filled with groceries.*	*Ingrid's stomach is in knots because she doesn't know if her mom will approve.*

2. What is mom's "surprise"? How does Ingrid feel about it?

She's pregnant. She feels dread because it's just another mouth to feed, and they don't have enough as it is.

3. **SHOWING VS. TELLING:** Instead of saying "We were very poor" (TELLING), Ingrid SHOWS their poverty through examples. List four details:

a. *The electricity gets turned off often.*

b. *The phone is always the first to go and her mom has a pay phone installed.*

c. *When their toilet breaks, they pee in the backyard garden or use the neighbor's toilet.*

d. *They never buy new clothes—all clothes are hand-me-downs or from the church thrift shop.*

Chapter 6

1. **DIALOGUE** (SCEDS) Identify the actions and emotional responses described during the dialogue between Ingrid and her dad regarding the divorce:

Event	What is said?	Blocking: What are the characters doing while they are talking?	What is the emotional response?
Dad calls Ingrid in to tell her about the divorce. (page 84)	Dad: "Well, Ingrid, your mother and I are getting a divorce."	*Her dad's hands are balled up into fists in his lap. His right fist is trembling. Ingrid slides her hand into his and squeezes it. He's in the living room, sitting on the green woven couch.*	*She's surprised at his sadness because he's never home anyway and he and her mom fight all the time.*
He explains the terms of what the divorce means for them. (page 85)	Dad: "If you ever love another man or call another man 'Dad,' you won't be my daughter."	*He sits upright with a serious face and stares at her hard.*	*She feels like she's been slapped. She's confused and her mind races.*

Name_____

CHAPTERS 5 & 6

Hippie Boy: (pages 63-86)

SCEDS FOCUS: DIALOGUE

Chapter 5

1. **DIALOGUE** (SCEDS) Identify the actions and emotional responses described with the dialogue during the grocery shopping scene:

Event	What is said?	Blocking: What are the characters doing while they are talking?	What is the emotional response?
Dad wants Ingrid and Connie to go grocery shopping. (page 63)	Dad: "Go get your shoes on. You two are doing the grocery shopping."		
Mom responds to Dad's demand. (page 64)	Mom: "Jerry, you can't let them do the grocery shopping. That money has to last us the entire month."		
Connie and Ingrid are at the Wonder Bread Outlet. (page 69)	Connie: "Look, Ingrid, ten loaves for one dollar. Mom is going to LOVE this."		
They return home with the groceries.	Dad: "Well, look at this. It looks like you girls did just fine. I knew you would."		

2. What is mom's "surprise"? How does Ingrid feel about it?

3. **SHOWING VS. TELLING:** Instead of saying "We were very poor" (TELLING), Ingrid SHOWS their poverty through examples. List four details:

   a.

   b.

   c.

   d.

Chapter 6

1. **DIALOGUE** (SCEDS) Identify the actions and emotional responses described during the dialogue between Ingrid and her dad regarding the divorce:

Event	What is said?	Blocking: What are the characters doing while they are talking?	What is the emotional response?
Dad calls Ingrid in to tell her about the divorce. (page 84)	Dad: "Well, Ingrid, your mother and I are getting a divorce."		
He explains the terms of what the divorce means for them. (page 85)	Dad: "If you ever love another man or call another man 'Dad,' you won't be my daughter."		

QUESTIONS FOR DISCUSSION/WRITING

1. Write a letter from Ingrid to her mom. Express how "you" (as Ingrid) truly feel about the pregnancy news.

2. Write a letter from Ingrid to her father. Express how "you" (as Ingrid) feel when he says you won't be his daughter if you call another man "dad."

3. What are your favorite/most despised meals? Who controls what you eat and how do you feel about it?

4. How has divorce impacted you?

CHAPTERS 7, 8, & 9 TEACHER'S GUIDE

Hippie Boy: (pages 87-126)

SCEDS FOCUS: NARRATOR EMOTIONS

Vocabulary:

implore (v)—*To beg for urgently.*

condescending (adj)—*Displaying a patronizingly superior attitude.*

defiance (n)—*Bold resistance to an opposing force or authority.*

mesmerize (v)—*To spellbind; enthrall.*

Chapter 7

1. Narrator **EMOTIONS** (SCEDS) Identify the emotional response described during the following events:

Event	What is Ingrid's emotional response to this event?
Dad changes after the divorce and is around a lot. He seems happier. (pages 87-88)	*She feels like she is going to burst from happiness. She loves it that he depends on her to fill him in on what happens at home and that he confides in her.*
Mom buys a car and starts dating. (pages 90-93)	*Ingrid is happy. It's fun to watch her mom act like a teenager. She is also proud of her for supporting them and even buying a car.*

Chapter 8

1. Narrator **EMOTIONS** (SCEDS) Identify the emotional response described during the following events:

Event	What is Ingrid's emotional response to this event?
Car accident (page 98) Phyllis: "Look at your face! It's covered in blood!"	*She can't focus; she thinks she's having a bad dream.*

Mom's boyfriend at the hospital. (page 100) Mom: "Ingrid, Karl's going to give you a blessing."	*Her mom's words hit her like a shock of electricity and a charge pumps through her body. She's not going to allow him near her and she panics.*
Ingrid's dad shows up. (page 102) "He entered the room carrying the most beautiful flower arrangement I had ever seen."	*Her heart dances. She realizes that he has not forgotten her.*
Ingrid sees her stitched-up face in the mirror. (page 103)	*She screams because she looks like a monster and cries herself to sleep that night. She also agrees to receive a blessing from the church elders.*

Chapter 9

1.   Narrator **EMOTIONS** (SCEDS) Identify the emotional response described during the following events:

Event	What is Ingrid's emotional response to this event?
They are ordered to take a "family" picture after Mom and Earl's temple marriage. (page 106)	*Her blood boils and she fights the urge to bolt out of the building.*
Ingrid's dad tells her she should have stood up to Earl and mom. (107)	*She wants to scream at him because he didn't stand up for her, but she holds it in.*
Mom tells the kids to call Earl "Father." (page 108).	*She looks around at everyone to make sure she heard correctly, then says "But he's not our father."*
Earl asks them about their day at the dinner table and Connie—at first—refuses to answer. (pages 111-112)	*Ingrid suppresses a laugh because she's impressed with Connie's will power. She feels that Connie is standing up for them.*
Ingrid's dad tells her about the bank's mistake in crediting him checks and how he talks his way out of it. (pages 120-122)	*Ingrid is proud that he is able to talk his way out of anything.*

Name_____

CHAPTERS 7, 8, & 9

Hippie Boy: (pages 87-126)

SCEDS FOCUS: NARRATOR EMOTIONS

Chapter 7

1. Narrator **EMOTIONS** (SCEDS) Identify the emotional response described during the following events:

Event	What is Ingrid's emotional response to this event?
Dad changes after the divorce and is around a lot. He seems happier. (pages 87-88)	
Mom buys a car and starts dating. (pages 90-93)	

Chapter 8

1. Narrator **EMOTIONS** (SCEDS) Identify the emotions, thoughts or reactions described during the following events:

Event	What is Ingrid's emotional response to this event?
Car accident (page 98) Phyllis: "Look at your face! It's covered in blood!"	
Mom's boyfriend at the hospital. (page 100) Mom: "Ingrid, Karl's going to give you a blessing."	
Ingrid's dad shows up. (page 102) "He entered the room carrying the most beautiful flower arrangement I had ever seen."	
Ingrid sees her stitched-up face in the mirror. (page 103)	

Chapter 9

1. Narrator **EMOTIONS** (SCEDS) Identify the emotions, thoughts or reactions described during the following events:

Event	What is Ingrid's emotional response to this event?
They are ordered to take a "family" picture after Mom and Earl's temple marriage. (page 106)	
Ingrid's dad tells her she should have stood up to Earl and mom. (page 107)	
Mom tells the kids to call Earl "Father." (page 108).	
Earl asks them about their day at the dinner table and Connie—at first—refuses to answer. (pages 111-112)	
Ingrid's dad tells her about the bank's mistake in crediting him checks and how he talks his way out of it. (pages 120-122)	

QUESTIONS FOR DISCUSSION/WRITING

1. Write a fantasy scene: describe how Ingrid and Connie want to respond to Earl at the dinner table when he asks them about their day.

2. When did you start to care about your appearance? What kind of clothes did you want to wear, what did you buy, what could you not afford to buy?

3. An accident or injury: how did it happen and how has it impacted your life?

4. Who do you fight with constantly? What issues come up over and over?

HIPPIE BOY SMALL SKETCH

Chapter Nine: At the Dinner Table (Ingrid, Mom, Earl, Connie)

Earl: Our Father, bless this food that my wife prepared for me, and bless this family that they will listen to my guidance and to the authority you have given me as priesthood holder. . .

Mom: Amen!

Earl: Connie, how was your day today?

(Connie ignores him.)

Earl: Connie! I asked you how your day was and you are going to answer me!

Mom: Connie, Earl asked you a question. Please answer him.

Connie: FINE!

Earl: WHAT did you just say to me? Tell your daughter to show me some respect! I'm warning you, do it NOW!

Connie: I don't need to put up with this. I'm out of here! (she stomps off. . .)

Chapters 10 & 11 Teacher's Guide

Hippie Boy: (pages 127-161)

FOCUS: SCENE CONSTRUCTION, STORY ARC

Vocabulary:

accentuate (v)—*Make more noticeable or prominent.*

perforated (adj)—*Having a hole or holes, especially a row of small holes.*

boomtown (n)—*A town that experiences a sudden growth in business and population.*

consignment (n)—*Goods shipped to a dealer who pays only for what is sold and who may return what is unsold.*

story arc (n)—*The purpose of a story arc is to move a character from one state to another; to effect change. This change or transformation often occurs when a character goes from a situation of weakness to one of strength.*

Chapter 10

1. **SCENE CONSTRUCTION**: Consider the following elements to identify the STORY ARC— what does Ingrid learn through the events of this scene?

   Scene, pages 127-132: Connie vs. Earl and the meeting with Bishop Jones.

   Scene opening: Earl rounds the corner with a mean smile on his face, insults Connie's dog and threatens to throw it out.

Component	
How does the scene opener set the stage for what is to come?	*When Earl insults Connie's dog, we know that Connie (most likely, given her love for animals) will not take it from him.*
What is the conflict?	*Earl vs. the kids, as usual and then Bishop Jones vs. the kids.*
How is this scene grounded in time and place? (What is the setting?)	*At first, Ingrid and Connie are in the living room folding laundry and later they are in Bishop Jones' office. He is towering over them, and it is hot and stuffy in his office (which accentuates Earl's stench).*

What is the context of this scene? What paragraphs add necessary background information for the present action to make sense? Are there any flashbacks?	*There is a paragraph describing Connie's love for animals and her ability to show affection for them (as opposed to people). There is also some background information given about Ingrid's mom's relationship with Bishop Jones—how she runs to him for advice about everything and how this had driven their Dad crazy when they were married. Also, that Connie and Ingrid think Bishop Jones is a hypocrite because they saw him drinking coffee.*
What action moves this scene along?	*Earl threatens Connie's dog and Connie threatens to leave. Earl throws her down on the rocking chair, but before he can hit, Connie kicks him in the face. At the meeting, Bishop Jones takes Mom's side and tells them they are lucky. When he talks to Ingrid and Connie alone, he tells them that their dad is no good. Connie questions him and walks out the door, Ingrid follows. They walk around for an hour before deciding to go home.*
How does the scene end?	*The girls return home and Connie is ready to defend their actions, but the house lights are off and they head to their rooms.*

Chapter 11

STORY ARC—Note how Ingrid's confidence grows as a result of the partnership between her and her father.

1. As Ingrid transitions from the dysfunction of her home life, identify how she reacts when her dad gives her responsibilities on the road:

How he offers Ingrid a partnership	How does Ingrid respond?
He shares his business plan with Ingrid and tells her he will be a millionaire someday.	*Her heart pounds with excitement at his plan and she encourages his dream.*
He hands her an atlas and names her the navigator.	*She feels proud to have a job, takes it seriously and plots their route through New Mexico and the Texas Panhandle.*
He asks her to help choose a place to live.	*She circles classified ads and searches for an apartment with a swimming pool. They look together and agree on a place.*
He asks for her help in setting up the house.	*She chooses all of the household items when they shop and sets it up at their apartment.*

2. After Ingrid gains confidence as her dad's partner, identify how he responds to her when she shows initiative:

Ingrid's initiative	How does her dad respond?
She tells her dad "I should be your sales organizer."	*He tells her he thinks she is "exactly right" and he pulls into a McDonald's so they can figure out the numbers.*
She asks for a notebook to keep track of money.	*He takes them to a 7-11 right after lunch to get one for her.*
She makes a rule that they can't stop for breakfast until they make their first $100, since that is the hardest part.	*He tells her she is made for this lifestyle.*
She realizes her most important job is keeping him encouraged and on target.	*Her encouragements are all it takes to reenergize him.*
When he tells her they need to increase sales, Ingrid decides that she needs to do some selling of her own.	*He tells her it's the best idea he's heard all day.*

3. **SETTING DESCRIPTION** (SCEDS): Identify the sensory details used to describe life on the road in the truck (page 154):

Visual	Auditory	Feel/Touch	Smell/Taste
By the end of the day, they are both sweaty and dirty. Hot dust kicked up at them when they stopped at the oil rigs to talk with prospects.	———	*The truck doesn't have air conditioning so she's covered in sweat and is constantly shifting to get comfortable.*	*Her dad cakes on Old Spice aftershave to hide his body odor.* *They celebrate the $100 sales mark with McDonald's Egg McMuffins and orange juice and lunch is usually a Hostess Cupcake and Sugar Free Dr. Pepper*

Name_____

Chapters 10 & 11

Hippie Boy: (pages 127-161)

FOCUS: SCENE CONSTRUCTION, STORY ARC

Chapter 10

1. **SCENE CONSTRUCTION**: Consider the following elements to identify the STORY ARC— what does Ingrid learn through the events of this scene?

    Scene, pages 127-132: Connie vs. Earl and the meeting with Bishop Jones.

    Scene opening: Earl rounds the corner with a mean smile on his face, insults Connie's dog and threatens to throw it out.

Component	
How does the scene opening set the stage for what is to come?	
What is the conflict?	
How is this scene grounded in time and place? (What is the setting?)	
What is the context of this scene? What paragraphs add necessary background information for the present action to make sense? Are there any flashbacks?	
What action moves this scene along?	
How does the scene end?	
What has been learned by Ingrid through the events of this scene?	

Chapter 11

STORY ARC—Note how Ingrid's confidence grows as a result of the partnership between her and her father.

1. As Ingrid transitions from the dysfunction of her home life, identify how she reacts when her dad gives her responsibilities on the road:

How he offers Ingrid a partnership:	How does Ingrid respond?
He shares his business plan with Ingrid and tells her he will be a millionaire someday.	
He hands her an atlas and names her the navigator.	
He asks her to help choose a place to live.	
He asks for her help in setting up the house.	

2. After Ingrid gains confidence as her dad's partner, identify how he responds to her when she shows initiative:

Ingrid's initiative:	How does her dad respond?
She tells her dad "I should be your sales organizer."	
She asks for a notebook to keep track of money.	
She makes a rule that they can't stop for breakfast until they make their first $100, since that is the hardest part.	
She realizes her most important job is keeping him encouraged and on target.	
When he tells her they need to increase sales, Ingrid decides that she needs to do some selling of her own.	

3. **SETTING DESCRIPTION** (SCEDS): Identify the sensory details used to describe life on the road in the truck (page 154):

Visual	Auditory	Feel/Touch	Smell/Taste

QUESTIONS FOR DISCUSSION/WRITING

1. What makes Ingrid transform from a situation of weakness to one of strength?

2. What happens to Ingrid and Connie's relationship through the Bishop Jones scene?

3. Ingrid's father buys a horse for his new stepdaughter. Write from Connie's point of view: how does she feel?

4. When has someone trusted you with adult responsibilities? How did that trust make you feel and how did you respond?

5. Ingrid and her father make a great team on the road. Who is your favorite "teammate" and why?

CHAPTERS 12 & 13 TEACHER'S GUIDE

Hippie Boy: (pages 162-201)

SCEDS FOCUS: CHARACTER, EMOTIONS and SETTING

Vocabulary:

dilemma (n)—*A situation that requires a choice between options that are equally unfavorable.*

summon (v)—*To request to appear; send for.*

harrowing (adj)—*Extremely distressing; agonizing.*

desolate (adj)—*Barren; lifeless.*

savvy (adj)—*Knowledgeable about the realities of life.*

rising action (n)—*The events of a narrative plot that lead up to the climax (where the character goes through a transformation).*

Chapter 12

1. **EMOTIONS** (SCEDS) Identify the emotions Ingrid describes when she is held down on the bed so that Earl can anoint her with sacred ointment to bless the evil spirits out of her:

Event	What is Ingrid feeling?	What happens to her physically as she experiences this emotion?
Ingrid has been called for her first "father/daughter meeting." (page 164)	She feels panicked.	*She feels the blood rushing to her face and her heart pounding too hard to relax.*
Ingrid's mom tells her that Earl is going to bless Satan out of her. (page 165)	She feels trapped.	*Her head pounds and their voices become a muffled jumble around her. She hears the word "Escape" come from inside of her.*

2. **SETTING DESCRIPTION** (SCEDS): Identify the sensory details used to describe the weed patch where Ingrid runs to hide after Earl tries to bless Satan out of her.

Visual	Auditory	Feel/Touch	Smell/Taste
It is a large, overgrown weed patch nearly the size of a football field. The weeds loom about four feet high.	*She hears her teeth chattering and the crickets chirping. She wants to hear her mom's voice calling to her.*	*She flattens the weeds, then plops down and hugs her knees to her chest. She rocks back and forth. She's freezing.*	_____

3. **CHARACTER DEVELOPMENT** (SCEDS): Ingrid's mother finally shows some backbone and stands up to Earl in this chapter. What happens?

   She tells Earl that it's more important for the kids to hear what happened to their dad than to read scriptures. She also tells him to wait when he wants breakfast.

Chapter 13

1. **CHARACTER DEVELOPMENT** (SCEDS): Ingrid gains some insight into her father while they are driving around. List four details about her father's past:

   a. *He grew up in a crowded shack with no indoor plumbing or electricity.*

   b. *He was one of eleven children and he started working on the farm when he was four.*

   c. *He was always tired from working so much, so he fell asleep at school and didn't do well.*

   d. *He could never play arcade games, go to movies, or eat ice cream because his family was too poor.*

2. Through hearing her dad's childhood stories, Ingrid shows some new understanding about him. What does she realize?

   She realizes that he'd felt like a slave as a child and that he was through being told what to do. That is where the need to be his own boss comes from.

3. Rising Action: Between pages 188-190, Earl's demands and actions escalate everyone's hatred for him. Name three things he does:

   a. *He decides he's the only one who can wear pants. He makes Ingrid's mom wear dresses all the time.*

   b. *He orders Ingrid's mom to fry up frog legs. When she refuses, he reads scriptures to her about obeying.*

   c. *He skins rabbits and hangs their bloody skins on the clothesline. Connie owns and loves rabbits.*

4. Why does Ingrid's mother slap her, and how does Ingrid feel in response?

   Ingrid's mother slaps her because she destroyed a "family" picture with Earl in it. (She colored over her face and poked a hold in the photo.) Ingrid feels like her heart has been ripped out because her mother considers slapping the worst thing someone can do to another person and she did it on Earl's behalf.

Name_____

Chapters 12 and 13 Pre-reading

1. **CHARACTER DEVELOPMENT** (SCEDS):

    Ingrid's dad is a magnet for trouble. In this chapter, an escaped convict holds him and his wife, Rhonda, hostage by gunpoint. Use at least seven of the following words to create a fictional story about what happens. (You are about to learn the true story):

    hotel

    gunman

    threatened

    gun

    cowering

    thin

    pale

    tall

    crazy

    high

    money

    blow

    trembling

    Chevy station wagon

    police officer

    handcuffed

    narrow

    dirt

    road

    battery cables

    wrench

    lights

    Las Vegas

Name_____

CHAPTERS 12 & 13

Hippie Boy: (pages 162-201)

FOCUS: CHARACTER, EMOTION, SETTING

Chapter 12

1. **EMOTIONS** (SCEDS) Identify the emotions Ingrid describes when she is held down on the bed so that Earl can anoint her with sacred ointment to bless the evil spirits out of her:

Event	What is Ingrid feeling?	What happens to her physically as she experiences this emotion?
Ingrid has been called for her first "father/daughter meeting." (page 164)	She feels panicked.	
Ingrid's mom tells her that Earl is going to bless Satan out of her. (page 165)	She feels trapped.	

2. **SETTING DESCRIPTION** (SCEDS): Identify the sensory details used to describe the weed patch where Ingrid runs to hide after Earl tries to bless Satan out of her.

Visual	Auditory	Feel/Touch	Smell/Taste

CHARACTER DEVELOPMENT (SCEDS): Ingrid's mother finally shows some backbone and stands up to Earl in this chapter. What happens?

Chapter 13

1. **CHARACTER DEVELOPMENT** (SCEDS): Ingrid gains some insight into her father while they are driving around. List four details about her father's past:

   a.

   b.

   c.

   d.

2. Through hearing her dad's childhood stories, Ingrid shows some new understanding about him. What does she realize?

3. Rising Action: Between pages 188-190, Earl's demands and actions escalate everyone's hatred for him. Name three things he does:

   a.

   b.

   c.

4. Why does Ingrid's mother slap her, and how does Ingrid feel in response?

QUESTIONS FOR DISCUSSION/WRITING

1. Why do you think Ingrid's mom stayed in the relationship with Earl even when she knew the marriage was having a devastating impact on her children?

2. Why did Ingrid feel so betrayed by her mother when she slapped her across the face? When have you felt a similar betrayal?

3. Ingrid destroys a "family" picture because Earl is in it and she gets slapped by her mother for it. When have you done something you knew was wrong but you had good reasons for doing it?

4. Ingrid finds an understanding teacher who allows her to hang out in his room after school. Who has been in the role of an unexpected ally for you?

HIPPIE BOY SMALL SKETCH

Chapter 12, Scene One: The Father/Daughter Meeting

(Characters: Ingrid, Mom, Earl)

Mom: We are going to start father/daughter talks. Ingrid, we are going to start with you.

Earl: Come on, Ingrid, let's go.

(they go to the bedroom)

Earl: First of all, I would like you to address me as "Father."

Ingrid: You are NOT my Dad!

Earl to Mom: Tell her to stop talking to me that way. Tell her. NOW!

Mom: Ingrid, stop it right now!

Ingrid: Just get away from me! Both of you!

Mom: Ingrid, listen to me. I think you have Satan inside of you. Earl's going to give you a blessing.

(They hold her down on the bed until Ingrid kicks Earl in the stomach and runs.)

Hippie Boy Small Sketch

Chapter 12, Scene Two: Kidnapped by a Gunman

(Characters: Dad, Rhonda, Police Officer, Gunman)

(Dad and Rhonda are at a hotel when their door is forced open and a gunman pushes a handcuffed police officer inside. He points the gun at Ingrid's dad. Rhonda runs into the bathroom and curls up into a shaking ball next to the toilet.)

Gunman: I'll blow your head off if you try anything!

Dad: Wait, I think I have some money here. **(He throws him $75.)**

Gunman (as he grabs money): Is anyone else in the room? **(He opens the bathroom door and sees Rhonda.)**

Gunman (to Rhonda): Get out here and sit on the bed! **(She sits next to the cop and Ingrid's dad.)**

Gunman (to Dad): Give me your car keys!

Dad: Go ahead and take the car.

Gunman: Shut up!

Gunman: Now here's what we're going to do. You are going to follow me quietly outside and we going to get in the car. If anyone says anything, I will blow your heads off!

Gunman (as he sees the beat-up Chevy station wagon): This is yours? This is a piece of shit!

Gunman: (after they get in the car) If I even see a police car, you're all dead!

Chapters 14 & 15 Teacher's Guide

Hippie Boy: (pages 202-240)

SCEDS FOCUS: ALL ELEMENTS

Vocabulary:

foreshadow (v)—*To show, indicate, or suggest in advance.*

climax (n) –*The turning point in a plot or dramatic action. Where the character changes and begins to solve the conflict.*

tirade (n)—*A long angry or violent speech.*

adjacent (adj)—*Next to; adjoining.*

extradite (v)—*To give up or deliver (a fugitive, for example) to the legal jurisdiction of another government or authority.*

embezzle (v)—*To take (money, for example) for one's own use in violation of a trust.*

Chapter 14

1. Ingrid is finally given a choice regarding where she will live. What does she decide and why?

    She decides to stay in the house because her younger siblings couldn't fend for themselves. She doesn't want Earl to get what he wants, either.

2. Ingrid's mother thinks they should take a family vacation without Earl in the summer. How does Ingrid respond?

    She's sad because she knows Earl will never let them go on their own.

3. Foreshadowing, event #1:

    a. Ingrid's dad has an idea for her involving his friend and a car. What is his idea, and what does he promise Ingrid?

    He wants her to drive a car to Iowa for his friend. He says he has a 1974 Volkswagen Super Beetle waiting for her, but it doesn't have an engine yet.

    b. Make a prediction regarding what will happen.

    Since Ingrid's dad is really good at making promises and not keeping them, it seems that this might be another similar situation.

4. Foreshadowing, event #2:

    a. After they trade in the van for a station wagon, Ingrid learns some surprising information from her dad. What does he tell her and what is his attitude about it?

    He left blank, signed checks with one of his sales guys, who wrote one out for $10,000 and cashed them at a bank. Now there was a warrant out for his arrest because his signature was on them. He tells Ingrid he's not concerned because he can get out of any situation. Plus, he didn't do anything wrong.

b. Make a prediction regarding what will happen.

He will get in trouble with the law and somehow get out of it. He always gets out of sticky situations.

5. Foreshadowing, event #3:

a. Ingrid's father gets a call at the hotel. Who is it?

Debbie, a telephone operator for AT&T, who called every Holiday Inn until she found Ingrid's dad.

b. Make a prediction about what will happen with Debbie.

Ingrid's dad and Debbie will get together. It's his pattern with women.

Chapter 15—PUT ALL OF THE SCEDS TOGETHER

1. **CHARACTER DESCRIPTION** (SCEDS): Identify the following sensory details Ingrid uses to describe herself in this chapter:

Visual What does she look like? What does she wear?	Auditory	Kinesthetic What is her body language? What are her facial expressions?	Smell
She has shoulder length hair, clear skin, and she wears mascara. *She wears shorts and a tank top.*	_____	*She brushes her tangled hair.*	*She uses Neutrogena face soap.*

2. **SETTING DESCRIPTION** (SCEDS): Identify the sensory details used to describe their early morning road trip:

Visual	Auditory	Feel/Touch	Smell/Taste
The sun sits on the fields before creeping up to the sky (personification).	*She loves the quietness as they drove, except for an occasional semi-truck. Willie Nelson's "On the Road Again" plays on the radio, they turn it up loud and sing along.*	*She loves the crisp, cool air. She tilts her head against the head rest and puts her arm out the window.*	_____

3. **DIALOGUE** (SCEDS) Identify the actions described during the dialogue in the following events:

Event	What is said?	Blocking: What are the characters doing while they are talking?
Ingrid and her dad are in the Plymouth, heading for Madison. (page 223)	Dad: "So what do you think, Ingrid?" Ingrid: "I think everything's great."	*He pats her leg as he speaks. She rolls down the window and the early morning air rushes against her face.*
They are pulled over by the officer. (page 225)	Dad: "Was I really going that fast? I'm sorry Officer. . ."	*He's smiling, but gripping the steering wheel with both hands and his knuckles are turning white.*
The officer finds her dad's fake ID. (page 228)	Dad: "I had that made up as a joke."	*His face is still being smashed against the trunk as he speaks.*

4. **EMOTIONS** (SCEDS) Identify the emotions described during the following events:

Event	What is Ingrid feeling?	What happens to her physically as she experiences this emotion?
She's waiting inside the car to find out the fate of her dad. (page 232)	*She feels miserable and anxious.*	*Her stomach is in knots and she has terrible diarrhea.*
Ingrid reads the note from her dad listing names of people she can call for money. (page 235)	*She feels stressed.*	*She feels like she's going to throw up.*
The judge says he's going to extradite her dad to Texas. (page 238)	*She feels shock and panic.*	*She feels like she has been scalded with a branding iron.*
Ingrid and her dad are back in the Plymouth, heading out again, and he doesn't thank her for saving him.	*She feels humiliated.*	*Her eyes sting from all of the crying. She looks out the window so he won't see the hurt on her face. A voice inside is screaming at her.*

5. **Climax**: What does Ingrid do at the court hearing? How does she change internally in this scene?

6. **SCENE CONSTRUCTION**: Consider the following elements to identify the STORY ARC—what does Ingrid learn through the events of this scene?

Scene, pages 225-240: Dad's arrest

Scene opening: Ingrid and her dad are on the road. They agree that "everything is great."

Component	
How does the scene opening set the stage for what is to come?	*By stating that everything is great, the reader has an idea that everything is not great—that something bad is about to happen.*
What is the conflict?	*Ingrid's dad is arrested because of his arrest warrant in Texas and faces imprisonment.*
How is this scene grounded in time and place? (What is the setting?)	*They are on the road from southern Illinois to Madison, Wisconsin. They are less than 200 miles from their destination.*
What is the context of this scene? What paragraphs add necessary background information for the present action to make sense? Are there any flashbacks?	*There is a paragraph reminding the reader of her father's arrest warrant in Texas, which is mentioned in chapter 14.*
What action moves this scene along?	*The arrest, Ingrid in the car alone, Ingrid receiving a note asking her to help him get the money he owes the bank, Ingrid seeing her dad in an orange jumpsuit, handcuffed and chained to others in a line, Ingrid watching the court proceedings and yelling "No!" when the judge says her dad will be extradited to Texas, the judge releasing him on a $5,000 fugitive bond in response to her protests.*
How does the scene end?	*When they are back in the car, Ingrid's dad doesn't thank her for saving him or ask how she survived the day. He proceeds as if nothing has happened. Ingrid feels humiliated and embarrassed.*
What has been learned by Ingrid through the events of this scene?	*Ingrid learns that her dad has stopped being the person who was always going to save her. He had become the person who needed to be saved.*

Name_____

Chapters 14 & 15

Hippie Boy: (pages 202-240)

SCEDS FOCUS: ALL ELEMENTS

Chapter 14

1. Ingrid is finally given a choice regarding where she will live. What does she decide and why?

2. Ingrid's mother thinks they should take a family vacation without Earl in the summer. How does Ingrid respond?

3. Foreshadowing, event #1:

    a. Ingrid's dad has an idea for her involving his friend and a car. What is his idea, and what does he promise Ingrid?

    b. Make a prediction regarding what will happen.

4. Foreshadowing, event #2:

    a. After they trade in the van for a station wagon, Ingrid learns some surprising information from her dad. What does he tell her and what is his attitude about it?

    b. Make a prediction regarding what will happen.

5. Foreshadowing, event #3:

    a. Ingrid's father gets a call at the hotel. Who is it?

    b. Make a prediction about what will happen with Debbie.

Chapter 15—PUT ALL OF THE SCEDS TOGETHER

1. **CHARACTER DESCRIPTION** (SCEDS): Identify the following sensory details Ingrid uses to describe herself in this chapter:

Visual What does she look like? What does she wear?	Auditory	Kinesthetic What is her body language? What are her facial expressions?	Smell

2. **SETTING DESCRIPTION** (SCEDS): Identify the sensory details used to describe their early morning road trip:

Visual	Auditory	Feel/Touch	Smell/Taste

3. **DIALOGUE** (SCEDS) Identify the actions described during the dialogue in the following events:

Event	What is said?	Blocking: What are the characters doing while they are talking?
Ingrid and her dad are in the Plymouth, heading for Madison. (page 223)	Dad: "So what do you think, Ingrid?" Ingrid: "I think everything's great."	
They are pulled over by the officer. (page 225)	Dad: "Was I really going that fast? I'm sorry Officer. . ."	

The officer finds her dad's fake ID. (page 228)	Dad: "I had that made up as a joke."	
When Ingrid speaks to her mom on the phone at the sheriff's office. (page 231)	Ingrid: "I'm fine. Everything's fine!"	

4. **EMOTIONS** (SCEDS) Identify the emotions described during the following events:

Event	What is Ingrid feeling?	What happens to her physically as she experiences this emotion?
She's waiting inside the car to find out the fate of her dad. (page 232)	She feels miserable and anxious.	
Ingrid reads the note from her dad listing names of people she can call for money. (page 235)	She feels stressed.	
The judge says he's going to extradite her dad to Texas. (page 238)	She feels shock and panic.	
Ingrid and her dad are back in the Plymouth, heading out again, and he doesn't thank her for saving him.	She feels humiliated.	

5. **Climax**: What does Ingrid do at the court hearing? How does she change internally in this scene?

6. **SCENE CONSTRUCTION**: Consider the following elements to identify the STORY ARC—what does Ingrid learn through the events of this scene?

Scene, pages 225-240: Dad's arrest

Scene opening: Ingrid and her dad are on the road. They agree that "everything is great."

Component	
How does the scene opening set the stage for what is to come?	
What is the conflict?	
How is this scene grounded in time and place? (What is the setting?)	
What is the context of this scene? What paragraphs add necessary background information for the present action to make sense? Are there any flashbacks?	
What action moves this scene along?	
How does the scene end?	
What has been learned by Ingrid through the events of this scene?	

Questions for Discussion/Writing

1. What kind of man is Jerry Ricks? What are his strengths and weaknesses? His flaws and contradictions?

2. Ingrid's dad has very high expectations for her. How do these expectations work in her favor? When are they too much?

3. What event changes everything for Ingrid? How is she different?

4. When have someone's expectations been too high for you? When have they been too low?

5. What event changed everything for you? How did you change as a result of that event?

Hippie Boy Small Sketch

Chapter Fifteen, Scene One: Ingrid and Dad Get Pulled Over (Ingrid, Dad, Police Officer)

Ingrid and her dad are in the car singing Willie Nelson's "On the Road Again" when he turns off the radio and looks into the rear view mirror.

Ingrid: Dad, what's going on? **(She looks, too, and sees flashing red lights.)**

Dad: What the hell was I thinking?

Dad (to officer): How you doin' officer?

Officer: Do you know how fast you were going?

Dad: I know I was going a little fast. I guess I wasn't paying attention.

Officer: Seventy-five miles per hour. That's twenty miles over the speed limit.

Dad: Was I really going that fast? I'm sorry, Officer. I didn't realize it.

Officer: Let me see your driver's license and registration.

Dad (after giving the officer his license): Ingrid, will you look in there and see if you can find the registration for me?

Dad (to Officer): I can't find the registration, but the car is registered, and we definitely have insurance.

Officer: Stay put. I'll be back in a minute.

(Officer comes back and holds a gun to the window, pointed at Dad's head.)

Dad: Oh shit!

Officer: Get your arms in the air and keep your hands where I can see them!

HIPPIE BOY SMALL SKETCH

Chapter 15, Scene Two: Ingrid Finds Her Voice (Ingrid, Dad, Man, Patrolman, Judge)

On her way into the courthouse, Ingrid sees her dad walking in a line of men wearing orange jumpsuits. Their hands are cuffed and they are connected to each other by a long chain wrapped around each of their waists.

Man: All rise. **(Ingrid sees her dad sitting in the front of the room.)**

Patrolman (to judge): This man has a warrant out for his arrest in Texas for embezzlement charges.

Judge (referring to Dad): Well, it looks like he should be extradited to Texas.

Ingrid (from the back of the courthouse): NO!

Judge: Who is this girl?

Dad: She's my daughter.

Judge (to Ingrid): Why don't you come up here? How old are you?

Ingrid: Sixteen.

Judge (to patrolman): Can you please explain what is going on here?

Patrolman: She was with him when I pulled him over.

Judge: Did you leave her alone all day sitting in a blazing hot car?

(Patrolman looks down, embarrassed.)

Judge (shakes his head in disgust and turns to Dad): Do you know how lucky you are to have a daughter who loves you so much?

Dad: Yes, I do Your Honor.

Judge: I am ordering that you be released on a five thousand dollar fugitive bond.

Dad and Ingrid: Thank you, Your Honor!

CHAPTERS 16, 17, & 18 TEACHER'S GUIDE

Hippie Boy: Chapters (pages 241-end)

FOCUS: Scene Construction

Vocabulary:

falling action (v)—*After the character changes during the climax, the events that take place to tie up the loose ends and bring the narrative story to a close is the falling action in the storyline.*

resolution (n)—*When the conflict has been resolved and the story has a finished, hopeful feel.*

Chapter 16

1. How does Ingrid reflect on what happened in the courtroom during the rest of their drive?

    She's thinking that everything has changed—that her dad was no longer the person who was always going to save her. She needs to save him now. She questions what might have happened if she hadn't intervened in the courtroom. It stings that he still hasn't asked her what happened to her while he was locked up.

2. **SCENE CONSTRUCTION:** Consider the following elements to identify the STORY ARC—what does Ingrid learn through the events of this scene?

    Scene, pages 253-268: Ingrid's solo road trip

    Scene opening: Ingrid suggests to her dad that she drive the Vega back to Utah.

Component	
How does the scene opener set the stage for what is to come?	*Now that Ingrid's dad respects her as a partner, it's clear that he's going to let her make the trip alone.*
What is the conflict?	*Ingrid is only 16—she hasn't been driving long and the car is unreliable. It's a long drive and her mother would not like this plan at all.*
How is this scene grounded in time and place? (What is the setting?)	*They are in Amarillo, Texas when she begins the road trip and she drives all the way to Logan, Utah.*

What is the context of this scene? What paragraphs add necessary background information for the present action to make sense? Are there any flashbacks?	*Ingrid reflects on many things while on the road: she describes her history with and appreciation for the white and yellow lines that stretch endlessly ahead of her, she looks forward to the surprise in store for her mom and Connie, she thinks more about how the arrest changed everything with her dad, and she thinks about the upcoming school year and how she is no longer afraid of Earl.*
What action moves this scene along?	*Ingrid's dad shows her all of the tricks to driving the car and Ingrid takes off on her own. She makes all of her own decisions on the road, but she does not call her dad at 4 pm like she was told; instead she calls him at 8 pm. He is furious and tells her to get a hotel right away.*
How does the scene end?	*When she pulls up to the house, Connie is impressed, her mom is furious and her dad is proud and impressed with her.*
What has been learned by Ingrid through the events of this scene?	*She has had the most perfect day of her life, and she had been responsible for every decision along the way. She has suddenly become independent.*

3. How does this scene show the change that has taken place within Ingrid?

After recognizing her independence from her dad during the court scene, she becomes more independent during this road trip.

Chapter 17

1. **FALLING ACTION**: Significant actions by each of the following characters tie up the loose ends of the story. Describe the interactions briefly and then identify Ingrid's reflections about what happened.

Character	What are this character's significant actions?	How does Ingrid reflect on or feel about this interaction?
Earl	*Earl slaps her mother and then gets into a physical fight with Ingrid. He leaves after Ingrid's mom tells him to, but is back within a few days. Ingrid tells her mother "If he stays, I go."*	*She transforms into the Incredible Hulk when she hears the slap. She feels good when she hits Earl. She is no longer afraid to stand up to him.*

Mom	*Mom finally asks Earl for a divorce after Connie sets up the meeting with Bishop Whitten.*	*Ingrid does not do a victory dance because she wants to show support to her mother. She tells her "I know things are going to get better now."*
Connie	*Connie tells Bishop Whitten what is going on so that he will tell her mom that it is okay to get a divorce. Her plan works.*	*She is floored that Connie has been able to orchestrate the whole thing. Relief washes over her. She wants to hug Connie through the phone.*
Dad	*Ingrid's dad tells her he is getting married and that Debbie will join him on the road.*	*She knows their days on the road have come to an end and she tells him, "She sounds like the perfect match for you." She is looking at her own future now.*

2. How do these reflections show Ingrid's growth as a character?

She shows strength and understanding in each situation. Before she would have responded with fear towards Earl and with less understanding for her mother and father.

Chapter 18—Resolution

1. What does the Beetle symbolize between Ingrid and her dad? What does it represent for Ingrid?

It symbolizes a fork in the road—that it is time to part ways. It represents freedom for Ingrid.

Epilogue

1. How has Ingrid's external conflict been resolved?

2. How has Ingrid's internal conflict been resolved?

Name_____

Chapters 16, 17, & 18

Hippie Boy: (pages 241-end)

Chapter 16

1. How does Ingrid reflect on what happened in the courtroom during the rest of their drive?

2. **SCENE CONSTRUCTION:** Consider the following elements to identify the STORY ARC— what does Ingrid learn through the events of this scene?

    Scene, pages 253-268: Ingrid's solo road trip

    Scene opening: Ingrid suggests to her dad that she drive the Vega back to Utah.

Component	
How does the scene opener set the stage for what is to come?	
What is the conflict?	
How is this scene grounded in time and place? (What is the setting?)	
What is the context of this scene? What paragraphs add necessary background information for the present action to make sense? Are there any flashbacks?	
What action moves this scene along?	
How does the scene end?	
What has been learned by Ingrid through the events of this scene?	

3.   How does this scene show the change that has taken place within Ingrid?

Chapter 17

1.   **FALLING ACTION:** Significant actions by each of the following characters tie up the loose ends of the story. Describe the interactions briefly and then identify Ingrid's reflections about what happened.

Character	What are this character's significant actions?	How does Ingrid reflect on or feel about this interaction?
Earl		
Mom		
Connie		
Dad		

2.   How do these reflections show Ingrid's growth as a character?

Chapter 18—Resolution

1.   What does the Beetle symbolize between Ingrid and her dad? What does it represent for Ingrid?

Epilogue

1. How has Ingrid's external conflict been resolved?

2. How has Ingrid's internal conflict been resolved?

Questions for Discussion/Writing

1. What hope do you have for Ingrid at the end of the book?

2. What strengths does Ingrid now possess that will help her reach her dream of going to college and having a successful life?

3. What character traits—both good and bad—did Ingrid inherit from her parents? How did these traits shape Ingrid's life?

4. Is the ending of the book satisfying or does it leave you hanging?

5. How is the conflict of the book resolved? How is it unresolved?

6. What is this book really about? What ideas are at its core?

Transformations

HOW WRITING MY STORY CHANGED MY LIFE

By Carolina Mooney—Author, "Bastard Child"

All my life I've had low self-esteem and tortured relationships with boys. I don't know my father, which has led me to engage in every form of self-destructive behavior possible. I've been promiscuous, constantly cheating on my significant others. I've never had a monogamous relationship that lasted longer than six months. Until now.

Last year, my high school English teacher gave me what I thought was yet another standard high school English assignment—a weekend's worth of work at most.

Boy, was I wrong. When I first wrote my piece, I didn't think much of it. It wasn't until I participated in a live interview on a local television show with two other authors from our book that I understood the full potential of our publication. We had written a self-help book for others while helping ourselves with our own healing process.

I originally decided to use a fake name for my story because I felt like I could hide behind it. The content of my story was extremely personal and graphic and covered things I didn't like to talk about with the closest of friends or even think about really. I was embarrassed and ashamed of my past and I felt that if I used a made up name, I wouldn't have to deal with the reality of the situation. My family knew nothing of the content of my piece other than the obvious part about me not having a father. Even then, they didn't know to which extent the lack of a father figure had affected me.

When my family ended up reading my story at our book release party, I felt violated and their reaction made me wish I hadn't written it. I had told them repeatedly that I didn't want them to read my piece and that if they did, I would be really angry. But how could I expect them not to? They were proud of me for having something published regardless of the content, and they were curious as to why I didn't want them to read it.

Although I was initially pissed off that they had read my story, it laid everything out on the table and forced us to talk about issues that really needed to be brought up. In doing so, it has changed my relationship with my family for the better.

While this experience was really difficult and exhausted me emotionally, if I ever had the chance to do something like this again, I definitely would. It was a great learning opportunity and I know that it has helped me immensely. I now realize that I need to own up to my past —that my past has made me who I am. I'm proud of what I've accomplished and since my secret is out, I no longer need to hide behind a pen name.

It's my hope that my story can continue to help others.

Read Carolina's story in *We Are Absolutely Not Okay: Fourteen Stories by Teenagers Who Are Picking Up the Pieces.*

TAKING DOWN ALL MY WALLS AND DEFENSES

By Leandra Hall—Author, "A Taste of the Real World"

When I first started writing about the time I ran away from home and encountered a man who forcefully begged me to have sex with him for money, the incident had already been on my mind for several weeks. Though four years had passed, I still couldn't get over it. Looking back on it made me feel violated and uncomfortable—sometimes even sending shivers down my back when I thought of it in detail.

I was skeptical about sharing my story at first. The idea that telling your story helps you get it off your chest and makes you feel better sounded like something your mom would say. But I decided to give it a shot and write about it in my English class. Sharing my experience with others was like taking down all of my walls and defenses, and allowing people I barely knew to see the hurt little girl who was hiding inside. At least that's how I felt.

When people started reading my story, they made me feel better about the incident by reminding me of how messed up a man that old must be to desire such a small young girl. They also made me feel good about myself when they praised my storytelling abilities. I'd never felt confident in reading or writing and always considered English my worst subject. But here were these adults and classmates telling me that I was actually good at it. It made me start to really enjoy writing—as long as it's in small portions.

As I stated briefly in my story, I went through a phase in my early teen years when I'd decided I could do whatever I wanted to do and didn't have to listen to my parents. As a result I got into some tangled situations that were pretty hard to get out of. I just want those who feel the same way I once did to realize that by refusing to listen, you can encounter a lot of danger and really get hurt. Rape and kidnapping really do happen. I've had to learn a lot of life's lessons the hard way and the thought of others having to do that is terrifying. I understand that not all may listen. But I hope that by sharing my story, at least a few will get it.

Read Leandra's story in *We Are Absolutely Not Okay: Fourteen Stories by Teenagers Who Are Picking Up the Pieces.*

THE EXPERIENCE OF A LIFETIME AND THE HEALING IT HAS BROUGHT ME

By Marika Evenson—Author, "The Monster within Him"

When Marjie gave us the assignment to write our stories in her English class, I cried. I just wanted to punch her. But after a good cry session, I changed my mind and decided to write mine. It's been very hard, but now I realize that this has been the experience of a lifetime.

I have always had problems with cutting and drugs and it has always tied back to the emptiness I've felt from not having my dad. Through this writing experience, though, I have healed more than I ever could have imagined. I started out hating myself and now have come around to loving myself.

Even though I hate what has happened to me in my life, it has made me who I am and I no longer want to change that. I don't think I would have ever felt that way fully without getting my story out. It has made me feel strong and has given me my power back.

We tell our stories hoping that they can help more than just us. I hope that you, too, will write your story and have your voice heard, because it is the most fulfilling feeling that you can experience.

Read Marika's story in *Behind Closed Doors: Stories from the Inside Out.*

FIGHT BACK METAPHORICALLY

By Maize Phillips –Author, "Loser, Failure, Dumbass"

This experience has helped me not only to understand my own struggles and how to overcome them, but also to understand the importance of not judging anyone by what they do, but instead finding out why they do it. It has helped to let my family know what I've been through, which has brought us even closer. Writing and sharing

my story has also helped motivate me to make better decisions and to succeed in school.

The negative motivation that these people gave me was the motivation to prove them wrong. I was tired of being labeled, and I wanted to be heard. When my voice was finally heard, I was overjoyed and was glad that my story could help so many people. People finally looked into my true being rather than discarding me as another teenager or as an idiot.

The writing process was rough. I wrote over twenty drafts total after working on my story for three months. But in the end, it was all worth it because writing and sharing my story has changed my perspective about other people. If anyone is struggling with this same situation, don't fight back physically or verbally; fight back metaphorically. You can do anything if you truly believe that you can, but you have to really believe in yourself. You cannot pretend to believe it. You can do it.

Read Maize's story in *Behind Closed Doors: Stories from the Inside Out.*

FINALLY ACCEPTING WHO I AM

By Brieaunna Dacruz — Author, "Closet Doors"

I learned so much from writing and publishing my story. When I was brainstorming what to write about, at first I didn't want to dwell on my past. But when I finally decided to share my story about coming out, it was one of the best decisions I have ever made. It helped me express what I have gone through in ways I never could before.

If you aren't accepted for who you are by others, don't let them break you. Stand up for yourself and stay strong. Nothing and no one is worth hiding your true identity. Coming out was the best decision I have ever made. It has brought me to where I am today and I couldn't be happier. My future has hope, things have gotten better, and I can now get through any obstacle that gets in my path.

Read Brieaunna's story in *Behind Closed Doors: Stories from the Inside Out.*

  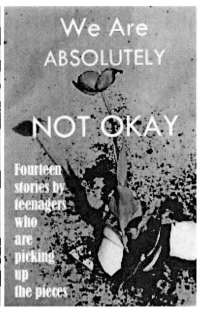

Purchase our books at:

Amazon (eBook/Paperback)
Barnes and Noble.com (Paperback)
Edmonds Book Shop (Paperback)

Please contact us for discounts on class sets.

www.WriteToRight.org

About Marjie Bowker

Marjie Bowker has taught English and a little history somewhere in the world for the past 18 years: in China, Norway and Vietnam, in addition to her "regular" spot at Scriber Lake High School, an alternative high school just north of Seattle, Washington. A strong advocate of community/student partnerships, she is constantly fostering relationships with community leaders to help enrich the lives of the teens she works with and was recently recognized as "Teacher of the Year" by the local VFW chapter for her innovative teaching/mentorship style. Past awards include a Paul Harris Fellowship Rotary Award and two NEH scholarships to study at Columbia University & Crow Canyon Archaeology Center. Marjie has traveled to more than thirty countries and is always on the lookout for creative ways to infuse her love of travel into her teaching career, including leading two trips to Costa Rica to save the Leatherback sea turtles.

About Ingrid Ricks

Ingrid Ricks is the author of The New York Times Bestseller *Hippie Boy*, which was recently acquired by Berkley, a division of Penguin Random House. She is also the author of Focus, a memoir about her journey with the blinding eye disease Retinitis Pigmentosa, and a short story collection, *A Little Book of Mormon (and Not So Mormon) Stories*. She is currently working on a memoir about her yearlong quest to heal her eyesight, and is blogging about her journey at www.determinedtosee.com. Ingrid's essays and stories have been featured on Salon and NPR. Along with writing, she is passionate about leveraging the new world of digital publishing to give teens a voice. For more information, visit: www.ingridricks.com.

CPSIA information can be obtained
at www.ICGtesting.com
Printed in the USA
FSOW02n1519131014
3234FS